The Eucharistic Revival Project

Edited by

Phillip Hadden & Jonathon Fessenden

Missio Dei

En Route Books and Media, LLC

Saint Louis, MO

⊕*ENROUTE*
Make the time

En Route Books and Media, LLC
5705 Rhodes Avenue
St. Louis, MO 63109

Contact us at **contact@enroutebooksandmedia.com**

Cover Credit: "The Holy Eucharist,"
usage rights purchased by contributor Dr. Joseph J. Plaud
from Restored Traditions website @ restoredtraditions.com

Copyright 2023 The Missio Dei Team

ISBN-13: 979-8-88870-071-6
Library of Congress Control Number: 2023945385

Table of Contents

Foreword

The Eucharist is the sacrament of sacraments, "the source and summit of the Christian life" (*Lumen gentium*, no. 11). As with all the other sacraments, it is an action of Christ through which the grace of the Holy Spirit enters our world and touches the human heart. It differs from the others, however, in that it brings not merely Christ's action into our world, but Christ Himself: Body, Blood, Soul, and Divinity. How this happens remains a mystery—but with God all things are possible (Lk 1:37).

The Greek word for "sacrament" is *Mysterion*, meaning "mystery." When we receive this mystery, Christ enters us and quietly transforms us into Himself as members of His Mystical Body. Centuries ago, St. Athanasius of Alexandria once wrote, "God became man so that man might become divine" (*On the Incarnation*, 54.3). The Eucharist is the primary means by which God brings this about. If Baptism makes us children of God, the Eucharist allows us to share ("participate in") the divine nature. Unlike normal bread and wine which become a part of us when we digest them, the Eucharist puts us in touch with the humanity and divinity of Christ Himself and allows us to intimately share in both.

This sacrament has three fundamental levels of meaning: banquet, sacrifice, and presence. When Jesus celebrated his Last Supper with his disciples, he instituted a New Passover meal, one in which He Himself became the sacrificial Lamb. As such, the Eucharist is an eschatological sign that points to the Messianic banquet that we will partake of in the world to come. This sacrament, however, is much more than a banquet, for Jesus' Last Supper was intimately connected with His sacrificial death. As such, it immerses us in a mysterious, unbloody way in that one sacrifice through which Christ offered His life for us to heal us of the wounds of the Fall, befriend us, and dwell within our hearts. We might even say that the Last Supper was not complete until Jesus said, "It is finished" (Jn 19:30, NRSV) as he hung from the cross and breathed his last breath. In addition to being a banquet and a sacrifice, the Eucharist is also a perennial sign of God's continuing presence in our lives. Jesus once said, "I am with you always, to the end of the age" (Mt 28:20, NRSV). When the priest utters the words, "This is my body" and "This is my blood" at the moment of consecration, the bread and wine are transformed, changed into the body and blood of Christ's glorified humanity. At every celebration of the Mass, Jesus enters our world anew and remains with us in the appearance of bread and wine. He lives in the tabernacle of every Catholic church, from the grandest cathedral to the humblest wayside chapel. He resides there to remind us that he loves us and will never abandon us, for he calls us his friends and wishes to dwell within our hearts.

"The paradise of God," St. Alphonsus de Liguori once wrote, "is the heart of man" (*The Way to Converse with God*, 1). When we receive the Eucharist we enter into a Holy Communion, a deep fellowship of friendship, with Jesus Christ, Our Lord and Savior. The purpose of the Eucharistic Revival going on in the Catholic Church in America today is to reignite our love and devotion for this wonderful gift from God. This collection of essays on the meaning and beauty of Eucharist is a welcomed contribution to this effort. I encourage all who come in contact with it to drink from the refreshing waters of this deep well.

Rev. Dennis J. Billy, C.Ss.R.
Robert F. Leavitt Distinguished Service Chair in Theology
St. Mary's Seminary & University
Baltimore, Maryland

About the Authors

Phillip Hadden lives in the Springfield Diocese in Illinois with his family. He holds a bachelor of arts in history with cum laude honors from the University of Illinois at Springfield and a Master of Arts in Theology—Sacred Scripture with summa cum laude honors from Holy Apostles College and Seminary. Phillip is the editor-in-chief of *Missio Dei LLC*. He lectors and teaches catechesis at his local parish. Phillip's interests include the Letters of St. Paul, St. Augustine, and covenant theology.

Kaleb Hammond is an undergraduate student in English and theology at Holy Apostles College and Seminary. He grew up in the rural foothills of the north Georgia mountains, but now lives just north of Indianapolis, Indiana. After a spiritual exodus from a nominally Protestant upbringing and a period of atheism, he converted to Catholicism through the influence of J.R.R. Tolkien and the study of philosophy, theology, and history, alongside his fellow-convert father. He has personally studied these subjects for many years and has written on them for his personal blog and for *Missio Dei*. Passionate about the pro-life cause, Catholic tradition, and the evangelization of culture, he plans to continue writing Catholic nonfiction and fiction and to pursue an academic career. In his spare time, he enjoys baseball, cooking, reading, and spending time with his family.

Chantal LaFortune is a writer for *Missio Dei* and the editor of several books for En Route Books and Media. She co-wrote and co-produced *The Song of Elbereth*, a radio play that aired on WCAT Radio. She enjoys writing poetry and has published several of her poems through the Society of Classical Poets. She will be completing her undergraduate studies at Holy Apostles College and Seminary in May 2024, double majoring in theology and English.

Fr. Chris Pietraszko is a Roman Catholic priest, in the Diocese of London, Ontario, Canada. He was ordained in 2012 to the priesthood, and continued to formally study the perennial Philosophy of St. Thomas Aquinas. He seeks to share the wisdom he gleans from this Doctor of the Church, and study it carefully. He has a devotion to the Eucharist as that was where he first encountered the Lord in a deeply personal, and transformative manner.

Dr. Joseph J. Plaud is a clinical and forensic psychologist. Additionally he has received his master of arts in theology degree from Saint Joseph's College in Standish, Maine. Dr. Plaud is enrolled in the doctor of theology program at Pontifex University in Atlanta, Georgia. He has been invested as a Knight in both the Equestrian Order of the Holy Sepulchre of Jerusalem and the Sovereign Military Hospitaller Order of Saint John of Jerusalem, of Rhodes and of Malta (Order of Malta) of the Roman Catholic Church. Dr. Plaud has also created and administers the website and online services for the Cathedral of SS. Peter and Paul in Providence, Rhode Island.

Fr. Dominic Rankin was ordained a priest for the diocese of Springfield, Illinois, in 2018 and completed his license in the theology of marriage and family at the John Paul II Institute in 2019. He has discovered in Pope St. John Paul II a mentor and model for priestly sanctity and a prophetic guide through the confusion and suffering present in our time.

Christina M. Sorrentino is a high school theology teacher and resides in the Archdiocese of New York in Staten Island. She earned her bachelor of science in biology and education through the Teacher Education Honors Academy and a master of science in education from the College of Staten Island. Additionally, she received a master teacher certificate in contemporary apologetics from Catholic Distance University and catechetical certification from the Archdiocese of New York. She is the author of poetry books entitled *Called to Love: A Listening Heart* and *Belonging to Christ*. Currently, Ms. Sorrentino is the editor-in-chief of *Ignitum Today* and has contributed to various publications including *Word on Fire*, *Homiletic & Pastoral Review*, *Catholic Exchange*, *Catholic Stand*, and *Missio Dei*. She has a deep and profound love for Jesus in the Eucharist and the priesthood of Jesus Christ, both at the center of her parish apostolates.

Kelly Ann Tallent, with a deep love for the Eucharist, crossed the Tiber River in December of 2005. Her love for Jesus is a grace given to her first and foremost by her parents' loving devotion to one another and to Him. It was deepened in Eucharistic Adoration through the example of her mother-in-law and father-in-law. Now, it is sacramentally lived in union with her wonderful spouse, Nehemiah. Their five children were the inspiration behind her initial authorship of *The Joyful Pessimist*, which was both a book and a blog. The writing journey continued as a contributor for Catholic Mom at Holy Cross Family Ministries. She is a graduate of Holy Apostles College and Seminary with degrees in both theology and English in the humanities, and she is currently the Coordinator for Youth and Family Formation for a parish cluster.

John Tuttle is a Catholic journalist, essayist, and blogger. Having graduated from Benedictine College with a bachelor of arts in journalism and mass communications and theology, his writing has appeared in *Catholic World Report*, *The Wanderer*, *Grotto Network*, *Starting Points Journal*, Franciscan Media, and *Tablet Magazine*, among others.

Joseph Tuttle is a Catholic writer and author who enjoys studying theology, liturgy, Sacred Scripture, the Catholicism of J.R.R. Tolkien, and the life and writings of Fulton J. Sheen. His work has been published with or is forthcoming with *Word on Fire Blog*, *Aleteia*, *Catholic World Report*, *Adoremus Bulletin*, *The University Bookman*, *The St. Austin Review*, *Homiletic and Pastoral Review*, *New Oxford Review*, *Voyage Comics Blog*, and *Missio Dei* among others. He is the author or editor of numerous books including *An Hour With Archbishop Fulton J. Sheen* (Liguori, 2021), *Tolkien and Faith: Essays on Christian Truth in Middle-Earth* (Voyage Comics, 2021), *The Stations of the Cross with Fr. John A. Hardon, S.J.* (Missio Dei, 2022) and *The Christbearer* (Voyage Comics, 2023) He graduated cum laude from Benedictine College with a Bachelor of Arts in Theology. He is currently pursuing a Master of Arts in Catholic Philosophical Studies at Saint Meinrad Seminary and School of Theology.

Chapter 1

Manna from Heaven

Kelly Ann Tallent

"This is how you are to eat it: with your loins girt, sandals on your feet and your staff in hand, you will eat it in a hurry. It is the Lord's Passover. For on this same night I will go through Egypt, striking down every firstborn in the land, human being and beast alike, and executing judgment on all the gods of Egypt—I, the Lord!"[1]

"But for you the blood will mark the houses where you are. Seeing the blood, I will pass over you; thereby, when I strike the land of Egypt, no destructive blow will come upon you."[2]

This is Israel's moment. After enduring enslavement for four-hundred and thirty years[3], they were going to walk out of Egypt and enter their Promised Land. God had given them signs and wonders, a holy leader, and a set of statutes that would eternally give glory to the One and only God who delivered them out of Egypt. Who could ask for a more glorious exit strategy?

---

[1] Ex. 12:10-11.
[2] Ex. 12:13.
[3] Ex. 12:41.

As the Israelites made their way out of Egypt, Pharaoh, in what seemed like a moment of clarity in grief, realized he was going to permanently lose his free manual labor. He rallied his armies and pursued the Israelites out into the desert. When the Israelites saw the six hundred chariots pinning them against the Red Sea, they cried out to God and to Moses:

> "Were there no burial places in Egypt that you brought us to die in the wilderness? What have you done to us, bringing us out of Egypt? Did we not tell you this in Egypt, when we said, 'Leave us alone that we may serve the Egyptians?' Far better for us to serve the Egyptians than to die in the wilderness." But Moses answered the people, "Do not fear! Stand your ground and see the victory the Lord will win for you today. For these Egyptians whom you see today you will never see again. The Lord will fight for you; you have only to keep still."[4]

As they stood there, terrified, Moses lifted his staff and his right hand, and God split the sea in two. The Israelites passed through the sea on dry land while the Egyptians slowly pursued, their chariots getting stuck in the wet bottom. Once the Israelites were safely on the other side of the sea, Moses again lifted his hand, and the sea returned, drowning the Egyptians and fulfilling Moses' prophetic promise of never seeing the Egyptians again.

---

[4] Ex. 14:11-13.

This deliverance drew out the victorious song from the relieved breath of the Israelites:

> I will sing to the Lord, for he is gloriously triumphant; horse and chariot he has cast into the sea. My strength and my refuge is the Lord, and he has become my savior. This is my God, I praise him; the God of my father, I extol him. The Lord is a warrior, Lord is his name! Pharaoh's chariots and army he hurled into the sea; the elite of his officers were drowned in the Red Sea. The flood waters covered them; they sank into the depths like a stone.[5]

One would like to imagine that the next sixteen hundred years consisted of the Israelites glorifying God and trusting Him, but that is not the case. Three days into the wilderness, they were out of water and grumbling against Moses. Two months and fifteen days into their eventual forty-year, self-induced exile,[6] the Israelites grumbled again, saying, "If only we had died at the Lord's hand in the land of Egypt, as we sat by our kettles of meat and ate our fill of bread! But you have led us into this wilderness to make this whole assembly die of famine!"[7]

The Israelite's lack of trust should not inspire indignation, but rather a deeper understanding of the human condition. They are a reflection of our own failings, but also a reflection of God's love for

---

[5] Ex. 15:1-5.
[6] Num. 14:34.
[7] Ex. 16:3.

His people. The Israelites were a nation called out by God as a prophetic example of God's love for the entire world. He did not leave
them to starve. "Then the Lord said to Moses: 'I am going to rain
down bread from heaven for you. Each day the people are to go out
and gather their daily portion; thus will I test them, to see whether
they follow my instructions or not.'"[8]

Just as the Lord did not leave the Israelites to die in the desert,
He did not leave the world to die as slaves to sin and death. As St.
Paul writes,

> But when the fullness of time had come, God sent his Son,
> born of a woman, born under the law, to ransom those under
> the law, so that we might receive adoption. As proof that you
> are children, God sent the spirit of his Son into our hearts,
> crying out, "Abba, Father!" So you are no longer a slave but
> a child, and if a child then also an heir, through God.[9]

As recorded in the Gospel of John, Jesus said:

> "Your ancestors ate the manna in the desert, but they died;
> this is the bread that comes down from heaven so that one
> may eat it and not die. I am the living bread that came down
> from heaven; whoever eats this bread will live forever; and
> the bread that I will give is my flesh for the life of the world."
> The Jews quarreled among themselves, saying, "How can

---

[8] Ex. 16:4.
[9] Gal. 4:4-7.

this man give us [his] flesh to eat?" Jesus said to them, "Amen, amen, I say to you, unless you eat the flesh of the Son of Man and drink his blood, you do not have life within you. Whoever eats my flesh and drinks my blood has eternal life, and I will raise him on the last day. For my flesh is true food, and my blood is true drink."[10]

Within these next chapters, the brothers and sisters of Missio Dei will be focusing on this new covenant through Jesus Christ. God provided the manna in the desert, which sustained the Israelites until they entered the Promised Land. Jesus provided His body and blood in this desert of life, which will sustain us until we enter our Promised Land—eternal life with our Beloved, our God and His Church. May God bless you and keep you, and may His face shine upon you—the face that shone on the creation of the world, on His people, on the Mother of His Son, and on "His Beloved Son in whom He is well pleased."[11]

---

[10] John 6:49-55.
[11] Matt. 3:17.

Chapter 2

The Fulfillment of Covenant

Phillip Hadden, MA in Theology—Sacred Scripture

Catholic and Jewish relations have suffered over time from acts of violence. In addition, contemporary society, which values diversity as its preeminent right, generally does not respect the concept of religious freedom. It's important, then, to make clear that Jesus of Nazareth in the New Testament is represented as the fulfillment of the prophecies made to the people of Israel and was crucified and resurrected for the salvation of everyone.

Since Jesus is presented by the New Testament as the fulfillment of the covenant with Israel, any notion within Catholic theology that attempts to apply a double truth like dual-covenant theory that causes resistance to evangelizing to the Jewish people must be rejected. Jesus is either the Jewish Messiah of whom the Jewish prophets spoke, or He is not. Jesus is either the Suffering Servant, or He is not. Jesus is either the eternal Davidic King, or He is not. The Church is made up of the generations of the children of Abraham, or it is not.

There is a twofold danger when discussing Catholic and Jewish relations from the Catholic perspective. There is danger in Christian theologians attempting to convey a quasi-dual-covenant theory that waters down the radicalness of the question posed by Jesus Christ,

"But who do you say that I am?"[1] The propositions that Jesus Christ is the true shepherd of Yahweh himself, prophesied in Ezekiel 34, and the Suffering Servant of the four servant songs found in Isaiah must either be affirmed or denied by the free choice of each person—a choice essential to their human dignity and religious freedom. The Commission for Religious Relations with the Jews released in 2015 a document called "The Gifts and the Calling of God Are Irrevocable," which explains:

> 34. That there can only be one history of God's covenant with mankind, and that consequently Israel is God's chosen and beloved people of the covenant which has never been repealed or revoked (cf. Rom 9:4; 11:29), is the conviction behind the Apostle Paul's passionate struggle with the dual fact that while the Old Covenant from God continues to be in force, Israel has not adopted the New Covenant.

It appears initially that with this particular paragraph from the Vatican Commission that the Jewish people's covenant is different from Christianity. However, the document makes a further clarification found in paragraph 35. It makes clear the danger of watering down the Christian claim of Jesus Christ being the sole mediator of the humanity and God, and no Catholic can claim otherwise.

> 35. Since God has never revoked his covenant with his people Israel, there cannot be different paths or approaches to

---

[1] Matt. 16:15.

God's salvation. The theory that there may be two different paths to salvation, the Jewish path without Christ and the path with the Christ, whom Christians believe is Jesus of Nazareth, would in fact endanger the foundations of Christian faith.... The Christian faith confesses that God wants to lead all people to salvation, that Jesus Christ is the universal mediator of salvation, and that there is no "other name under heaven given to the human race by which we are to be saved" (Acts 4:12).

The second danger from the Catholic perspective is to disregard and ignore the history of Catholic and Jewish relations as one filled with prejudice that ignores the atrocities committed by either the Church or individual Catholics toward the Jewish people. David Kertzer, in his book on anti-Semitism and the Catholic Church titled *The Popes Against the Jews*, writes,

Although various histories of the fraught relations between the Roman Catholic Church and the Jews have been published, most focus on a more remote past. Others examine Church doctrine, engage in biblical exegesis, or analyze various other texts, and so do not capture the actual struggle between the Church and the Jews.[2]

---

[2] David Kertzer, *The Popes Against the Jews* (New York: Vintage Books Group, 2002), Introduction, Kindle Edition.

The historic struggle between the Jewish people and the Catholic Church is important because it does need to be acknowledged as a vital issue that causes strain in any dialogue, even dialogue focused primarily on the theological and on biblical exegesis. Kertzer explains that mistreatment of the Jewish people by Catholics in the nineteenth century was the catalyst that led to the easy acceptance of German Nazi genocide by many European Christians on the continent. Kertzer explains this treatment by focusing on a particular example used in the French Catholic publication *La Civiltà Cattolica*:

> Jews battled the Church, that they practiced the ritual murder of Christian children, that they had enormous political power in their hands to the point of controlling governments and, above all, that they possessed great wealth, earned by usury, and thus had incredibly strong economic influence, which they used to the detriment of Christianity and Christian peoples.[3]

Kertzer gives countless evidence of these examples, including the precursor of the yellow Star of David patch the Jews were forced to wear in Nazi occupied territories, explaining, "Jews in the Papal States were still being prosecuted in the nineteenth century when caught without the required yellow badge on their clothes, mandated by Church councils for over six hundred years."[4]

---

[3] Ibid.
[4] Ibid.

The examination of history is important here because Kertzer uses these examples to criticize the 1998 Vatican Commission for Religious Relations with Jews document "We Remember: A Reflection on the Shoah," which seeks to make a distinction between anti-Judaism and antisemitism found in Church history. He says, "the distinction made in the report between 'anti-Judaism'—of which some unnamed and misinformed Christians were unfortunately guilty in the past—and 'anti-Semitism,' which led to the horrors of the Holocaust, will simply not survive historical scrutiny."[5] Kertzer points out that the prejudices exampled in the quote from the French magazine run far deeper than simply anti-Judaism, but are inherently tied to both culture, or rather cult, and is so tied to a particular race of people. It's extremely important for both Catholic historians and theologians to listen to and to acknowledge this point. The importance of doing so is that it can be fruitful to then present a primarily theological and exegetical argument for the Jewish people to accept Jesus of Nazareth as the Messiah. If the Church can show humility, then it may be possible to make a proposition that isn't anti-Judaist or antisemitic.

The point is conveyed very well in paragraphs 30 and 31 of "The Gifts and the Calling of God Are Irrevocable:"

This Christological exegesis can easily give rise to the impression that Christians consider the New Testament not only as the fulfilment of the Old but at the same time as a replacement for it. That this impression cannot be correct is

---

[5] Ibid.

evident already from the fact that Judaism too found itself compelled to adopt a new reading of Scripture after the catastrophe of the destruction of the Second Temple in the year 70.[6]

In some sense, the document points to an alike historic development of Christianity and Rabbinic Judaism, as it is a development from Second Temple Judaism. Unfortunately, the misunderstanding of a dual-covenant theory by culturally sensitive theologians is a reaction to centuries of Jewish discrimination found in the West, namely on the European continent, which especially gained more ground within academia due to the catalyst of the horrendous holocaust on the Jewish people. Although a reaction out of compassion, the result of such a development in popularity in dual-covenant theory has caused another form of antisemitism, one of theological segregation: the Jews have their own relationship with God, and Christian have their own covenant. Naturally, the application of the prophetic literature, especially that found in the major prophets, repudiates such a reading as exemplified in the standard prophetic message: 1. Israel/Judah has broken the covenant and better repent; 2. No repentance? Then judgment to Israel/Judah and the Nations; 3. Restoration for Israel/Judah and the nations.[7] It is the application of

---

[6] Commission for Religious Relations with the Jews. (2015, December 10). *The Gifts and the Calling of God Are Irrevocable (Rom 11:29)*. Catholicculture.org. Online at https://catholicculture.org/culture/library/view.cfm ?recnum=11101

[7] J. Daniel Hays, *The Message of the Prophets* (Grand Rapids: Zondervan, 2010), 63.

the standard prophetic message and especially focusing on the third part, where the restoration by Yahweh is a gathering of the people of Israel and the Gentile nations into a single covenant.

The Catholic (Christian) Debate on Creation, Covenant, and Evangelization

The Catholic exegesis acknowledges that Christ is the sole mediator of salvation, so the Catholic question of God's relationship with humanity is primarily a question of soteriology, which, perhaps, differs from the ends of Jewish covenantal exegesis tied to a land and its people. Therefore, the Catholic theologian cannot separate the philosophical, historical, and theological from the question of what the purpose or end of man is, because God has acted in history through His revelation moving toward the restoration of humanity. Therefore, in the Christian perspective, God's creation now is moving toward a linear end times and renewal, and attempts to rectify this revealed truth with St. Paul's teaching found in Romans 11:29, which is quoted verbatim in the title of the 2015 Vatican document "The Gifts and the Calling of God Are Irrevocable," must be fully acknowledged as this perspective is either true for all people or not. Paragraphs 34 and 35 of the document makes it clear that there cannot be a dual covenant; however, paragraph 36 leaves the question open for the work of theologians, which has led to the confusing proposition that the Jews cannot be evangelized and that they will be saved without the Church:

36. From the Christian confession that there can be only one
path to salvation, however, it does not in any way follow that
the Jews are excluded from God's salvation because they do
not believe in Jesus Christ as the Messiah of Israel and the
Son of God. Such a claim would find no support in the sote-
riological understanding of Saint Paul, who in the Letter to
the Romans not only gives expression to his conviction that
there can be no breach in the history of salvation, but that
salvation comes from the Jews ... Just as decisively he asserts:
"For the gifts and the call of God are irrevocable" (Rom
11:29). That the Jews are participants in God's salvation is
theologically unquestionable, but how that can be possible
without confessing Christ explicitly, is and remains an un-
fathomable divine mystery.

At this point there can be some room for debate, St. Paul's teaching of God's covenant with the people of Israel especially, in lieu of
Romans 11:26, "And in this way all Israel will be saved," is a fairly
debated text among theologians of both covenantal and dispensa-
tionalism theologies. Benjamin Merkle, in his book *Discontinuity to
Continuity: A Survey of Dispensational & Covenantal Theologies*, explains that there is no particular consensus to be found within the
frameworks of continuity in covenant theology:

Similar to progressive covenantalism, there is no consistent
interpretation of Romans 11:26 offered by covenant theologians. The identity of "Israel" in Paul's phrase, "And in this
way all Israel will be saved," is understood to refer to (1) the

church, (2) the elect among ethnic Israel throughout history, or (3) a future mass conversion of ethnic Israel.[8]

The debate has led to some heated debates even into the early twenty-first century. Professor Philip Cunningham of Boston College offered a response to the esteemed Catholic theologian Avery Cardinal Dulles' support of the single covenant fulfilled by Jesus Christ in an article printed in 2002 in *America* magazine. In the article, Cunningham asserts, "our interfaith group, half of whom are Catholic scholars, asserts that Christians should not seek to convert Jews: In view of our conviction that Jews are in an eternal covenant with God, we renounce missionary efforts directed at converting Jews. At the same time, we welcome opportunities for Jews and Christians to bear witness to their respective experiences of God's saving ways."[9] Cunningham goes onto to explain, "In other words, dialogue, not conversion, should be the Catholic goal in relations with Jews."[10]

Cunningham's overall criticism of Dulles' opinion on the covenant of Israel being fulfilled by Jesus Christ, and, therefore in need of the gospel of Christ's salvation, is mostly based on Dulles' critiques given of a document called "Reflections on Covenant and

---

[8] Benjamin L. Merkle, *Discontinuity to Continuity: A Survey of Dispensational & Covenantal Theologies* (Bellingham, WA: Lexham Press, 2020), 160.

[9] Philip A. Cunningham, "Theology's Sacred Obligation," *America*, modified December 9, 2012. Online at https://www.americamagazine.org/issue/ 408/article/theologys-sacred-obligation

[10] Ibid.

Mission." "Reflections" was produced by the Bishops' Committee on Ecumenical and Interreligious Affairs and the National Council of Synagogues on August 12, 2002.[11] Cunningham also invokes the teaching of the Catholic Church since the Vatican II council invoked the council document *Nostra Aetate*, which is the Second Vatican council's *Declaration on the Relationship of the Church to Non-Christian Religions*. The Christian covenant is the continuity of the covenant of the people of Israel, into which they will be grafted back and in which there has been no consensus on how this grafting will take place.

Cunningham rightly critiques Dulles' opinion of relying too much on the New Testament writings when he says,

> Much of Cardinal Dulles's critique of these concepts in *Reflections* flows from his reading of the New Testament... we are troubled by Cardinal Dulles's assertion that the Letter to the Hebrews offers "the most formal statement of the status of the Sinai Covenant under Christianity." Without further analysis, he quotes Hebrews: The "first covenant is 'obsolete' and 'ready to vanish away.'"[12]

Naturally, this type of analysis can read a bit harsh to the ears of our Jewish friends, and it can seem to relegate them to the margins. It must be stressed that rather being obsolete, Christianity is founded on Judaism, which includes them, and both it and they are

---

[11] Ibid.
[12] Ibid.

vital to its mission in the world—without the chosen people of Israel, without their Messiah, who Christians claim is Jesus Christ, Christianity cannot exist in a vacuum without its Jewish roots.

So, the question remains, after the most recent Vatican document on Jewish relations and the Vatican II council documents, *Nostra Aetate* and *Lumen Gentium*: should Catholics evangelize Jews? Rather, should it be put in this manner, if Jesus is the Messiah, the Suffering Servant of Israel and the Shepherd of Ezekiel of Jewish prophecy, would this not be an injustice to segregate the cult away from its people, as Kertzer accuses the Vatican of doing in his historical analysis? Catholic theologian Ralph Martin explains that the idea of not evangelizing the world, which includes the Jews, is simply a misreading of the mission of Vatican II. *Lumen Gentium*, paragraph 16, contains a vital footnote with its statement, Martin explains:

> The text first explains how "those who have not yet received the Gospel are related to the People of God in various ways." A footnote here references a text from St. Thomas, *ST* III, q. 8, a. 3, ad 1: "Those who are unbaptized, though not actually in the Church, are in the Church potentially. And this potentiality is rooted in two things—first and principally, in the power of Christ, which is sufficient for the salvation of the whole human race; secondly, in free-will." It is clear that this "relatedness" **is not actually salvific, but potentially salvific** (emphasis my own). Special mention is made first of the Jews, then of the Muslims, and then of unspecified other

religions and peoples.... The text then affirms God's universal salvific will, citing 1 Timothy 2:4 as a basis for its exploration of how salvation for those who do not know the gospel
might be possible.[13]

What Martin understands in this particular debate is that the
Christian view of covenant is one of soteriology. In the Gospel of
Matthew chapter 28, Jesus gives His disciples, primarily Jews, a man-
date that also includes the immediate Jewish population: "Go therefore and make disciples of all nations, baptizing them in the name of
the Father and of the Son and of the Holy Spirit, teaching them to
observe all that I have commanded you. And behold, I am with you
always, to the end of the age." [14] In the next section, a proposition
will be laid out similar to the patristic period of the Church that the
major prophets conclude that Mosaic covenant is broken and ended;
however, it begs some explanation that the minor prophets do inform the people of Israel returned from exile to continue to follow
the law of Moses, as they are still waiting for the fulfillment of the
promised restoration. Hays, notes in his reading of Haggai, Zecha-
riah, and Malachi that "the return to the Land after the exile hardly
signaled a return of the days of blessing in the Promise Land...Even
though they did rebuild the temple, there is no mention of Yahweh
coming in spectacular fashion to dwell in the temple, as he did when

---

[13] Ralph Martin, *Will Many Be Saved?: What Vatican II Actually
Teaches and Its Implications for the New Evangelization* (Grand Rapids,
MI; Cambridge, U.K.: William B. Eerdmans Publishing Company, 2012),
7–8.

[14] Matt. 28:19-20.

Solomon finished the first one."[15] In fact, the narrative account of the return from exile in the book of Ezra records the building of the second temple and also give no account and is silent on Yahweh returning to the temple. The minor prophets, also known as a complete unit of the "book of the twelve," end then with this understanding of keeping the law:

> "Remember the law of my servant Moses, the statutes and rules that I commanded him at Horeb for all Israel. Behold, I will send you Elijah the prophet before the great and awesome day of the Lord comes. And he will turn the hearts of fathers to their children and the hearts of children to their fathers, lest I come and strike the land with a decree of utter destruction."[16]

It's therefore important in continuity with this prophetic understanding that in the Gospel accounts, Jesus of Nazareth claims that John the Baptist comes in the spirit of Elijah, thus marking the beginning of the fulfillment of the new covenant to which the major prophets point:

> As they went away, Jesus began to speak to the crowds concerning John: "What did you go out into the wilderness to see? A reed shaken by the wind? What then did you go out to see? A man dressed in soft clothing? Behold, those who

---

[15] Hays, *The Message of the Prophets*, 344.
[16] Mal. 4:4-6.

wear soft clothing are in kings' houses. What then did you go out to see? A prophet? Yes, I tell you, and more than a prophet. This is he of whom it is written,

> 'Behold, I send my messenger before your face,
> who will prepare your way before you.'

Truly, I say to you, among those born of women there has arisen no one greater than John the Baptist. Yet the one who is least in the kingdom of heaven is greater than he. From the days of John the Baptist until now the kingdom of heaven has suffered violence, and the violent take it by force. For all the Prophets and the Law prophesied until John, and if you are willing to accept it, he is Elijah who is to come. He who has ears to hear, let him hear."[17]

Jesus the Messiah and the Jewish Prophetic Witness of Fulfillment

Biblical exegesis, in an attempt to come to the proper conclusion of this question, needs to also include the prophetic canon of both Jewish and Christian Sacred Scripture. It is the canon that surrounds the Babylonian exile, mainly the major prophets, examined with the particular language found in Romans 11, that is needed to come to an understanding of what St. Paul means by Israel and who will be part of the new covenant found in Christ Jesus, prophesized by the major prophets Isaiah, Jeremiah, and Ezekiel.

---

[17] Matt. 11:7-15.

Why the prophets? Jesus of Nazareth explains the history of the people of Israel to the chief priests and Pharisees in a parable found in the Gospel of Matthew about a master of a house who owned a vineyard and gave commands to procure the fruits of the seasons harvest. The commands of the master of the house were given to his servants, who were beaten, stoned, and killed by the workers of the vineyard who the master had entrusted as his stewards of his land. Of course, Jesus is recounting to the chief priests and pharisees salvation history. He relies on the prophets such as Moses, Isaiah, Jeremiah, Ezekiel and others to affirm that the landowner, who is God, has entered into a covenantal agreement with his people and wishes to procure the fruits such a covenant. The workers of the vineyard have decided to attempt to elevate their status by rejecting obedience to the master by killing the heir of the master's land. Jesus explains the effect of such actions taken by the workers:

"When, therefore, the owner of the vineyard comes, what will he do to those tenants? They said to him, 'He will put those wretches to a miserable death and let out the vineyard to other tenants who will give him the fruits in their seasons.'"[18]

Jesus then explains to the chief priests and pharisees that this vineyard is the kingdom of God, which will be taken away from them and given to a people who will produce fruits for the glory of the Master. Jesus says:

---

[18] Matt. 21:40-41.

"Therefore I tell you, the Kingdom of God will be taken away from you and given to a people producing its fruits."[19]

If we're to accept Cunningham's conclusion not to evangelize the Jews, then the parable loses its commonsense teaching to the chief priests and Pharisees. It seems Martin's reading is the correct view, that the Jewish people are included in the new covenant prophesized in both the Jewish and Christian canon of prophets. If Martin's view (and Dulles') is the one to be accepted and not Cunningham's, then there needs to be a way to reconcile Roman 11:26-29 with such an understanding. Catholic theologians Brant Pitre, Michael Barber, and John Kincaid, in a co-authored book, give an answer to what exactly is the meaning of St. Paul's words found in Romans 11:26.

> For one thing, if we want to know what Paul means when he says that "all Israel [*Israēl*] will be saved [*sōthēsetai*]" (Rom 11:26), it is critical to interpret it within the broader context of Romans 9–11. Here Paul has already declared that "not all who are descended from Israel [*Israēl*] belong to Israel" (Rom 9:6 RSV). With these words, he reduces "true" Israel to "those who put their faith in Christ." Moreover, Paul explicitly anchors his expectation of "Israel" being "saved" in Isaiah's prophecy that "only a remnant [*hypoleimma*] of them will be saved [*sōthēsetai*]" (Rom 9:27). This strongly suggests that he does not expect every individual Israelite to

---

[19] Matt. 21:43.

be saved. Instead, Paul thinks that at some point in the future there will be a conversion of the full number of the elect remnant that will reveal that God has not rejected Israel.[20]

It is clear from the exegesis here that simple dialogue, and not evangelization, with the Jewish people proposed by Cunningham would not fit with St. Paul's meaning found in Romans chapter 11. The analysis also agrees with option two presented in Merkle's book on covenant theology quoted earlier. In 2005, Avery Cardinal Dulles explains that the documents of the Vatican II council do not insist on simple dialogue with the Jewish people, because it is inconsistent with the council's teaching found in *Lumen Gentium* of the faithful's obligation to spread the faith. Dulles explains, "Christ gave the apostles, and through them the Church, the solemn commission to preach the saving truth of the gospel even to the ends of the earth: 'The obligation of spreading the faith is imposed on every disciple of Christ, according to his ability,' as *Lumen Gentium* puts it."[21] Dulles explains precisely what the council and further developments after the council have sought to clarify:

The Second Vatican Council, while providing a solid and traditional framework for discussing Jewish-Christian

---

[20] Brant Pitre, Michael P. Barber, and John A. Kincaid, *Paul, a New Covenant Jew: Rethinking Pauline Theology* (Grand Rapids, MI: William B. Eerdmans Publishing Company, 2019), 28–29.

[21] Avery Cardinal Dulles, "The Covenant With Israel: Avery Cardinal Dulles," *First Things*, last modified November 1, 2005. Online at https://firstthings.com/ article/2005/11/the-covenant-with-israel.

relations, did not attempt to settle all questions. In particular, it left open the question whether the Old Covenant remains in force today...

In the half-century since Vatican II major contributions to Catholic covenant theology have been made by Pope John Paul II, Joseph Cardinal Ratzinger (now Pope Benedict XVI), Walter Cardinal Kasper, the *Catechism of the Catholic Church,* and the Pontifical Biblical Commission. With these contributions, together with some less authoritative writings, we may find a path through the thickets of controversy.[22]

Dulles makes an important distinction in the covenant history of Israel. He explains that there are many covenants made with the people of Israel: Noah, Abraham, Moses, and David. He observes that these particular covenants are not all equal with each other. Dulles explains:

The term "covenant" is the usual translation of the Hebrew *b'rith* and the Greek *diatheke*. Scholars commonly distinguish between two types of covenant, the covenant grant and the covenant treaty. The covenant grant, modeled on the free royal decree, is an unconditional divine gift and is usually understood to be irrevocable.... The prime example of a conditional covenant is that of Sinai, as interpreted in the Deuteronomic tradition. It promises blessings on those who

---

[22] Ibid.

observe its conditions and curses on those who violate them (see, for example, Deuteronomy 30:15-20).[23]

Dulles answers the challenge from Cunningham that he relies too much on the New Testament by explaining that the Mosaic covenant, the covenant of atonement for sins, the covenant of the law was conditional, and it was broken by the people of Israel. The importance of this particular understanding is that by examining the major prophets and the text surrounding Babylonian exile, the canon shared by both Jews and Christian acknowledges the condition of the Mosaic covenant, it being broken, and a new covenant that will replace this broken covenant. It further gives explanation to a disturbing phrase by God found in Ezekiel 20:25: "Moreover, I gave them statutes that were not good and rules by which they could not have life, and I defiled them through their very gifts in their offering up all their firstborn, that I might devastate them. I did it that they might know that I am the Lord. [24]

The covenant of the law could not give life; the sacrifices of the people of Israel could not truly cleanse their sins. Dulles' exegesis on the Letter to the Hebrews explains this odd Ezekiel passage very well in reference to the old practices found under the covenant of the law:

Those who treat the Old Covenant as dead and superseded are generally thinking of its legal prescriptions, especially those connected with worship, as treated in the Letters of

---

[23] Ibid.
[24] Ezek. 20:25.

Paul and the Letter to the Hebrews.... The Letter to the Hebrews, which is essentially a treatise on priesthood, teaches that with the cessation of the Levitical priesthood and the Temple sacrifices, the Old Covenant is to that extent superseded: "For where there is a change in the priesthood, there is necessarily a change of law as well."[25]

So this begs the question: can it be certain that the Mosaic covenant ended? What can the canon that is shared by both Jews and Christian explain to us? Perhaps the easiest place to start is the ending of the covenant with the people of Israel, found in the book of the prophet Jeremiah, chapter 11, verses 9-17:

> Again the Lord said to me, "A conspiracy exists among the men of Judah and the inhabitants of Jerusalem. They have turned back to the iniquities of their forefathers, who refused to hear my words. They have gone after other gods to serve them. **The house of Israel and the house of Judah have broken my covenant that I made with their fathers.** Therefore, thus says the Lord, Behold, I am bringing disaster upon them that they cannot escape. Though they cry to me, I will not listen to them. Then the cities of Judah and the inhabitants of Jerusalem will go and cry to the gods to whom they make offerings, but they cannot save them in the time of their trouble. For your gods have become as many as your cities, O

---

[25] Dulles, "The Covenant With Israel," *First Things*.

Judah, and as many as the streets of Jerusalem are the altars you have set up to shame, altars to make offerings to Baal.

"Therefore do not pray for this people, or lift up a cry or prayer on their behalf, for I will not listen when they call to me in the time of their trouble. What right has my beloved in my house, when she has done many vile deeds? Can even sacrificial flesh avert your doom? Can you then exult? The Lord once called you 'a green olive tree, beautiful with good fruit.' But with the roar of a great tempest he will set fire to it, and its branches will be consumed. The Lord of hosts, who planted you, has decreed disaster against you, because of the evil that the house of Israel and the house of Judah have done, provoking me to anger by making offerings to Baal."[26]

J. Daniel Hays, professor of Old Testament at Ouachita Baptist University, explains the particular language used in Jeremiah 11 and its ramifications:

The Hebrew word translated as "broken" does not carry a mere connotation of "to violate" as when we break the law today, say, by speeding; it implies breaking the relationship, as in an annulment.... In Jeremiah 11 Yahweh declares that Israel and Judah have broken (ended) the Mosaic covenant,

---

[26] Jer. 11:1-17.

thus setting up the need for a "new" covenant, as presented in Jeremiah 31.[27]

The *Navarre Bible* commentary explains,

The prophetic literature points quite often to end of Mosaic covenant by implication of either a reversal of the Exodus narrative as found in the book of the prophet Jeremiah 41-43:

> The Lord has said to you, O remnant of Judah, 'Do not go to Egypt.' Know for a certainty that I have warned you this day.[28]

> Now therefore know for a certainty that you shall die by the sword, by famine, and by pestilence in the place where you desire to go to live." [29]

Or framing the coming of the Messiah as a new Exodus event in the history of the people of Israel, which includes all nations found in the book of the Prophet Isaiah:

> In that day the root of Jesse, who shall stand as a signal for the peoples—of him shall the nations inquire, and his resting place shall be glorious.

---

[27] Hays, *The Message of the Prophets*, 163.
[28] Jer. 42:19.
[29] Jer. 42:22.

In that day the Lord will extend his hand yet a second time to recover the remnant that remains of his people, from Assyria, from Egypt, from Pathros, from Cush, from Elam, from Shinar, from Hamath, and from the coastlands of the sea.

He will raise a signal for the nations and will assemble the banished of Israel, and gather the dispersed of Judah from the four corners of the earth.

The jealousy of Ephraim shall depart, and those who harass Judah shall be cut off; Ephraim shall not be jealous of Judah, and Judah shall not harass Ephraim.

But they shall swoop down on the shoulder of the Philistines in the west, and together they shall plunder the people of the east.

They shall put out their hand against Edom and Moab, and the Ammonites shall obey them. And the Lord will utterly destroy the tongue of the Sea of Egypt, and will wave his hand over the River with his scorching breath, and strike it into seven channels, and he will lead people across in sandals.

And there will be a highway from Assyria for the remnant that remains of his people, as there was for Israel when they came up from the land of Egypt. [30]

The *Navarre Bible* commentary gives a wonderful explanation if it is to be understood that the second option of Merkle's explanation

---

[30] Isa. 11:10-16.

(and Catholic theologians Pitre, Barber, and Kincaid) on what St. Paul means with the Jewish people being grafted back into the olive tree in the continuity of covenantal theology,

> a "remnant" will return in triumph and joy to the land that God gave them. The four stanzas in this passage look forward to "that day" thereby setting the glorious fulfilment of the promises of salvation in an eschatological context.... The Church sees herself in this "remnant" who have experienced God's salvation and she feels called to bear witness to her joy before all mankind. "Therefore," says Vatican II, "all sons of the Church should have a lively awareness of their responsibility to the world; they should foster in themselves a truly catholic spirit; they should spend their forces in the work of evangelization."[31]

The remnant, which is the Church, also includes the elect of the Jewish people chosen by God through His invitation to the divine life by His covenantal promises.

Isaiah, Jeremiah, and Ezekiel continually point toward the fact that restoration of God will include peoples outside of the people of Israel. Therefore, the proposition that Israel must have a separate agreement outside of Christian covenantal theology or other nations not only is prejudice on the grounds of excluding the Jewish people from the affirmative of the closed question of whether Jesus is their

---

[31] James Gavigan, Brian McCarthy, and Thomas McGovern, eds., *Major Prophets*, The Navarre Bible (Dublin; New York: Four Courts Press; Scepter Publishers, 2005), 90.

Messiah or not, but also doesn't relate to the commonsense message of the canon text. In those particular texts, the Christian proposes that Jesus is the "Suffering Servant" of Isaiah (Isaiah 40-53), He is the new covenant restoration of the Davidic King (Jeremiah 31-33), and He is Yahweh as the Good Shepherd (Ezekiel 34). The proposition that Christ is the fulfillment of Jewish prophecy is the foundational Catholic understanding of the role of the major prophets as the witness of the fulfillment of God's covenant with humanity, stemming from Adam to Christ. St. Augustine writes in the *City of God*, quoting Isaiah 10:22:

> And it is their own Scriptures that bear witness that it is not we who are the inventors of the prophecies touching Christ. That is why many of them, who pondered these prophecies before His passion and more especially after His Resurrection, have come to believe in Him, as was foretold: "For if thy people, O Israel, shall be as the sand of the sea, a remnant of them shall be converted."[32]

The Christian, therefore, makes the claim that Jesus fulfills these vital Jewish prophecies that fulfill the eternal covenants that Avery Cardinal Dulles explains are still in continuation. Jesus is either who He says He is, or He is not (or what Christians claim and profess

---

[32] Augustine of Hippo, *The City of God, Books XVII–XXII*, ed. Hermigild Dressler, trans. Gerald G. Walsh and Daniel J. Honan, vol. 24, The Fathers of the Church (Washington, DC: The Catholic University of America Press, 1954), 164.

Him to be). The question proposed is because these prophecies and covenants originate from the Jewish people, for the sake of the dignity of their persons, if Christians hold Jesus to be the fulfillment of Jewish prophecy, is the Christian obligated to inform the Jewish people? If Christians are who we claim to be then the answer must be, "yes," or we forfeit our reward. What must be avoided is the negative sentiments expressed toward the Jewish people in the same tone used by St. Augustine in the same section of *City of God* and other Church fathers that reflect the prejudices of their time and culture. However, such a rejection of rhetoric does not render the application of patristic exegesis with illuminating the fulfillment of Jewish prophecy in Christ Jesus; this can still be accepted as the correct reading with a critique on prejudices that existed during the period.

The New Covenant of Jeremiah

The people of Israel have broken the covenant with God, after they had been warned the consequences of doing so in Deuteronomy 28. Again, what are the consequences? They are a reversal of the Exodus motif on the people of Israel:

> The Lord will strike you with the boils of Egypt, and
> with tumors and scabs and itch, of which you cannot
> be healed. The Lord will strike you with madness and
> blindness and confusion of mind, and you shall

grope at noonday, as the blind grope in darkness, and
you shall not prosper in your ways.[33]

Hays explains that, "In Jeremiah 11 Yahweh declares that Israel
and Judah have broken (ended) the Mosaic covenant, thus setting
up the need for a "new covenant, as presented in Jeremiah 31."[34] Jeremiah 31 is fairly commonly known, as Jesus Christ would take up
these themes and language at the Last Supper with instituting a new
sacrifice before His Passion on the cross and death. The book of the
prophet Jeremiah is engrained into the very actions of Jesus
throughout the Gospels. Jesus' actions such as His first miracle at the
wedding at Cana, or his recounting of the many wedding parables,
are a sign that He has come to reverse the curses of Deuteronomy
28.[35]

In fact, it is during the celebration of old Exodus of the Passover,
where Jesus establishes a new meal of commemoration for the new
Exodus, which is His body and blood as the sacrificial victim, explained in more detail in the servant section of Isaiah. This meal,
with its connection to Jeremiah 31, establishes the new covenant
with Israel and the Gentile peoples just as it was foretold God would
do by the major prophets.

---

[33] Deut. 28:27-29, ESVCE.

[34] J. Daniel Hays, *The Message of the Prophets* (Grand Rapids: Zondervan, 2010), 163.

[35] Ibid, 165.

"Behold, the days are coming," declares the Lord, "when **I will make a new covenant** with the house of Israel and the house of Judah, **not like the covenant** that I made with their fathers on the day when I took them by the hand to bring them **out of the land of Egypt, my covenant that they broke**, though I was their husband," declares the Lord. "For this is the covenant that I will make with the house of Israel after those days," declares the Lord: "I will put my law within them, **and I will write it on their hearts**. And I will be their God, and they shall be my people."[36]

There are several things to touch on with this particular passage of Jeremiah. The first is the prophecy of the establishment of a new covenant. The second is the return of the theme of the ending of the Mosaic covenant by an Exodus reversal or a new Exodus motif, and, finally, this covenant will be written on the hearts of God's people. There is an interesting aspect with having the law written in one's heart. Hays notes, "in the Hebrew of the Old Testament the term 'heart' usually refers to one's 'seat of volition.' That is, one's heart is where one makes decisions, especially whether to follow Yahweh in obedience or not."[37] The tragedy of the dual-covenant theory is simple with this understanding. It's founded on a sense of religious indifference, *not sensitivity*, because if Jesus is the Messiah, if that's the truth, then leaders and theologians of the Church who actively try to prevent this good news from hearers who ought to hear are

---

[36] Jer. 31:31-33, ESV.

[37] J. Daniel Hays, *The Message of the Prophets* (Grand Rapids: Zondervan, 2010), 180.

committing a serious infraction of the new covenant established by God, by actively refraining from proposing Jesus to the Jewish people.

The Suffering Servant of Isaiah

The reference to the Suffering Servant of Israel almost always invokes chapter 53 in Isaiah. There are four passages (or songs) though that refer to this servant of Israel in Isaiah, including chapter 53. The first servant song found in chapter 42 sets the foundation for the role of the servant who will come in the spirit of Yahweh himself:

> Behold my servant, whom I uphold,
> my chosen, in whom my soul delights;
> I have put my Spirit upon him;
> he will bring forth justice to the nations.[38]

It's also important to note that this language of the spirit of Yahweh is used throughout the book of Isaiah. In fact, Jesus reads from the book of the prophet Isaiah chapter 61 in the beginning of His ministry in reference to the spirit of Yahweh and concludes that through Him this prophecy is fulfilled:

> And he rolled up the scroll and gave it back to the attendant and sat down. And the eyes of all in the synagogue were fixed on him. And he began to say to them, "Today this Scripture

---

[38] Isa. 42:1.

has been fulfilled in your hearing." And all spoke well of him and marveled at the gracious words that were coming from his mouth. And they said, "Is not this Joseph's son?"[39]

Discussion about new covenant theology or continuity usually surrounds the new covenant theme found chapters 31-33 of the prophet Jeremiah. However, new covenant language is very active throughout the second section of Isaiah, as is the idea of a new exodus. The new Exodus motif in relationship with the new covenant strike both the seriousness of what Isaiah is describing throughout the servant songs, which is the development of Israel's covenant relationship with God, that includes the suffering servant who comes in the spirit of Yahweh.

In the first servant song, Isaiah speaks very directly about this new covenant. The new covenant will include the Gentile peoples. Hays explains,

the first Servant song, stresses that the coming Servant will have the Spirit of Yahweh and will establish justice on the earth with all the nations...the Servant will be quite and meek.... Yahweh tells the Servant that he has called him in righteousness and will make him a "covenant for the people and a light for the Gentiles (nations)."[40]

---

[39] Luke 4:20–22.

[40] J. Daniel Hays, *The Message of the Prophets* (Grand Rapids: Zondervan, 2010), 125.

If there is a possibility of a dual-covenant theory, or rather a two-fold approach of single covenant, it exists under this understanding of the Spirit of Yahweh and God's anointed one. John Bergsma's book titled *Jesus and the Dead Sea Scrolls: Revealing the Jewish Roots of Christianity* examines the Qumran and Essenes perspective of the coming messiah in relation to many of these particular prophecies. Bergsman explains that passages read by Essenes were taken quite literally. The Qumran community, Bergsman claims, had a messiah-like figure who founded their community, known as the "teacher of righteousness." Bergsman writes, "Many scholars think this Teacher was the high priest in Jerusalem who was forced out by the Maccabean King Jonathan Applius… the legitimate High Priest was then exiled and founded the community by the Dead Sea."[41] The interesting part is that there is this interesting phrase in a particular document of the Qumran community known as the *Damascus Document*:

> They shall not be reckoned among the council of the people, and their names shall not be written in their book from the day the Beloved teacher dies until the Messiah from Aaron and from Israel appears.[42]

The most significant aspect of the second servant song of Isaiah is the mission or role the servant will play in this new covenant. The

---

[41] John Bergsma, *Jesus and the Dead Sea Scrolls: Revealing the Jewish Roots of Christianity* (New York: Image, 2019), 16.

[42] Ibid, 17.

second servant song in some ways plays well into the previously discussed intention of what exactly is to be understood by the grafting back into the olive tree of the people of Israel in St. Paul in Romans 11 and the irrevocableness of God's gifts. He says:

> "It is too light a thing that you should be my servant
> to raise up the tribes of Jacob
> and to bring back the preserved of Israel;
> I will make you as a light for the nations,
> that my salvation may reach to the end of the earth."[43]

There are a couple points of discussion with the concept of mission in the second servant song. In the beginning of chapter 49, it refers to the servant with reference to "Israel," so some commentators have suggested that it's a corporate understanding with this particular song. The *Navarre Bible* commentary addresses this point by asserting that such claims are made with little textual evidence:

> The mention of Israel does not argue against the servant's being an individual rather than a collectivity, for in poetry a person can be addressed by his own name or by his family name. In fact, both in biblical Israel and nowadays we often find people using their place of birth as a surname.[44]

---

[43] Isa. 49:6.

[44] *Major Prophets*, The Navarre Bible, 216.

The *Navarre* commentary also gives another good explanation in reference to what is to be understood as the mission of the servant of Israel. Although the means to its arrival through the people of Israel isn't understood, it will be made more clear with the last servant song, or rather, the Suffering Servant Song.

> In vv. 5–6 the Lord spells out the servant's mission: it is to renew the people in such a way that even non-Israelites can see the light and attain salvation. Although the universal mission of the servant is not clearly defined here, for his work is meant to be confined to the tribes of Jacob, still the achievement of this objective (the reassembling of Israel) will be a kind of light to help the pagan nations see and acknowledge God. The expression "light to the nations" (v. 6) already occurred in the earlier poem (42:6); there it could be taken in a social sense—to bring about the liberation of the exiles and captives; here, the religious meaning is clear: salvation will spread to all the nations."[45]

So is there a twofold covenant understanding of the Messiah that could fit into a prophetic Messiah for the people of Israel and a kingly Messiah in Jesus? It's not likely, as indicated by the *Navarre* commentary. In the Essene understanding of the messiahship of prophet and king, Jesus by his gesture of sitting and teaching takes on the prophetic messiahship as well as the Davidic. Bergsma notes on the particular scene where Jesus quotes Isaiah 61,

---

[45] Ibid, 216.

There was tension in the air, because he had just read a passage that all Jews considered significant…. What will Jesus say about this passage? "I am the one Isaiah is describing here: the one anointed by Lord to proclaim the jubilee and restore Israel. I am the fulfillment of the passage."[46]

The text in Isaiah shows a clear mission that the new covenant that is forged by this servant in the first servant song is not in any way two separate missions or covenants, but rather it is a single covenant, a single visible mission of the second person Jesus. The third servant song of Isaiah focuses on the emergence of a new Exodus, a new covenant, and therefore, a new starting point with Israel's relationship with God. The third song, as explained by Hays, indicates a position that the new covenant through the servant does not have a temporal salvation, but rather an eternal component to its overall theme. The servant expresses his trust in God, as Hays writes: " Numerous earlier themes reappear: New Exodus motifs, justice and righteousness, comfort for Jerusalem, Yahweh as powerful creator, the eternal nature of Yahweh's salvation in contrast to humanity's temporal nature."[47]

Finally, the fourth song, known as the "Suffering Servant song," is the centerpiece of Christian understanding of the messiah found in the prophetic literature. Pope Benedict XVI explains:

[46] John Bergsma, *Jesus and the Dead Sea Scrolls: Revealing the Jewish Roots of Christianity* (New York: Image, 2019), 25.

[47] J. Daniel Hays, *The Message of the Prophets* (Grand Rapids: Zondervan, 2010), 128.

The Song of the Suffering Servant in Isaiah compares the suffering servant of God with the lamb that is led to the slaughter: "Like a sheep that before its shearers is dumb, so he opened not his mouth" (Is 53:7). Even more importantly, Jesus was crucified on the feast of the Passover, and from that moment on could only appear as the true Passover lamb, in whom is fulfilled the significance of the Passover lamb at the time of the Exodus from Egypt: liberation from the dominion of death in Egypt and release for the Exodus, for the journey into the freedom of the promise. In light of Easter, this lamb symbolism takes on a fundamental importance for understanding Christ.[48]

Pope Benedict XVI notes the identity of the Suffering Servant is wrapped up in Jesus Christ. Again, it gets to the fundamental question of Jesus: "Who do you say that I am?" If Jesus Christ is the suffering servant, then he is the cornerstone of the Jewish covenant with God. The eternal covenants and the new covenant established after the ending of the mosaic covenant are fulfilled in the person of Jesus Christ. He is either the servant whom the spirit of Yahweh is upon, or He is not—there can be no, yes He is for Christians, and no He isn't for Jews. It is a question out of the dignity of freedom that must be addressed.

---

[48] Benedict XVI, *Jesus of Nazareth: From the Baptism in the Jordan to the Transfiguration.* Trans. by Adrian J. Walker. (New York: Double Day, 2007).

Chapter 3

St. Paul and the Lord's Supper

Phillip Hadden, MA in Theology—Sacred Scripture

"Do this, as often as you drink it, in remembrance of me."
For as often as you eat this bread and drink the cup, you pro-
claim the death of the Lord until he comes. [1]

If the Catholic faithful are to have a revival of the source and summit of our faith—the Eucharist—then the faithful must have a firm understanding of the first known tradition of the form of the Eucharist understood by St. Paul in the context of what Paul refers to as the Lord's Supper. The narrative of the Passion account in the Synoptic Gospels describes intimately the institution of the Eucharist by Jesus within the setting of the Passover meal and the Mosaic covenant of Israel; however, the Synoptic narratives are not the earliest New Testament tradition of the Eucharist's institution. The earliest tradition of the Eucharist is found in St. Paul's First Letter to the Corinthians. Fr. Raymond F. Collins dates the oral tradition of St. Paul's account prior to circa 51 A.D.[2] Collins explains,

---

[1] 1 Cor. 11:25–26, NABRE.

[2] Raymond F. Collins, *First Corinthians*, ed. Daniel J. Harrington, vol. 7, Sacra Pagina Series (Collegeville, MN: The Liturgical Press, 1999), 425.

1 Corinthians 11:23–26 contains the oldest literary account of the Last Supper. The account antedates the letter. Paul's introduction reminds the Corinthians that the account is something he had previously shared with them, presumably at the time of his visit to them in the middle of the first century c.e. The tradition is older than that.[3]

The First Letter to the Corinthians by St. Paul is essential for understanding the early background for the development of the form of the Eucharistic rite. It is fashionable among biblical scholars to develop hypotheses about early Christianity, such as the *Jesus Seminar*, in which the New Testament is the product of oral traditions developed within the early communities. The primary issue with these hypotheses is an attempt to critique the written record via textual criticisms, primarily redaction criticism, for the purpose of building hypotheses on the early Christian communities based on intuition instead of relying on the written record, which, in fact, is not a discipline of history. Redaction criticism does have its uses when properly employed in certain circumstances; however, the biblical texts accepted in their final form, like the Corinthian letters written by St. Paul, are and remain the most detailed historical accounts of the day-to-day life of early Christian communities.[4]

It's important to stress that the biblical interpretation of this chapter does not claim to be the only interpretation of these passages found in the First Letter to the Corinthians. It is the view of the

---

[3] Ibid.

[4] Charles B. Puskas and Mark Reasoner, *The Letters of Paul: An Introduction* (Collegeville: Liturgical Press, 2013), 89.

author that Sacred Scripture is the living Word of God, so it still actively speaks to Christians today. However, it is also the view that any interpretation of the text cannot be stretched past its authorial intentions and its own historical contexts—both are considered in my exegesis here. Bible readers may find some differences in their own interpretation, but that's to be expected when it comes to interpreting Sacred Scripture. The interpretation of Sacred Scripture is like the layers peeled from an onion. James V. Brownson explains, "plurality in interpretations not necessarily a sign of interpretive failure, but often of interpretive effectiveness, reflecting a distinctive convergence of the text with the particular context of the reader."[5] The interpretation expressed here focuses on minimizing existing divisions in our own Catholic circles as understood by the charisms of Missio Dei itself: proclamation of the gospel and unity among those who proclaim it.

A Survey of Corinth in First Century A.D.

The consensus of early twentieth century biblical scholars suggested that factionalism in the church of Corinth was the occasion or reason for St. Paul's letter to the Corinthians. N.T. Wright and Michael Bird describe, "More likely, many of the problems were coloured, if not directly caused, by the intense factionalism within the small Corinthian church, reflecting the competitive culture of

---

[5] James V. Brownson, *Speaking the Truth in Love: New Testament Resources for a Missional Hermeneutic* (Harrisburg: Trinity Press International, 1998), 15.

rivalry and personality politics that was nasty but normal in Corinth."[6]

Fr. Raymond Collins suggests that the modern consensus has shifted in the overall opinion of what life was like for those who lived in Corinth in the first century A.D. The consensus of scholars in the early twentieth century believed that the divisions expressed by St. Paul in his First Letter to the Corinthians were primarily driven by factions. Fr. Collins explains:

> "Early twentieth-century commentators often expressed the view that the basic problem in Corinth was factionalism, with various segments of the Christian community rallying around the name of one or another Christian hero—Apollos or Cephas, Paul, or even Christ himself…. Paul, however, does not seem so much to have addressed himself to particular groups as to have dealt with particular issues as he developed the argumentation of his letter."[7]

One key feature that Fr. Collins suggests is St. Paul doesn't address groups within his letter, so the text of the letter itself eliminates factionalism as a root cause for divisions among the Corinthians, so what could possibly be the source for these existing divisions within the early Christian community in Corinth? One aspect that Wright

---

[6] N. T. Wright and Michael F. Bird, *The New Testament in Its World: An Introduction to the History, Literature, and Theology of the First Christians* (London; Grand Rapids, MI: Zondervan Academic; SPCK, 2019), 480.

[7] Collins, *First Corinthians*, 16.

and Bird suggest is what they describe as a "culture of personal loyalties" and "generating bickering."[8] The cause for divisions in first century Corinth appears to be caused by the diversity of social class and stratum. The more affluent Christians had more opportunities available to them in their daily activities. For example, rich patrons would own larger homes for feasts. In the context of First Corinthians, the more affluent patrons were gathered in the banquet hall, while those who showed up later in the evening like laborers and slaves would be restricted in the atrium after dinner had commenced. St. Paul's letters provide textual evidence throughout Corinth of social stratification. The driving factor for the context of St. Paul's rebuke and treatment of the Lord's Supper in chapter 11 is the division between the rich and poor.

The concern for ancient writers, typically in the function of letter writers such as St. Paul, is the occasion that causes the purpose for the letter to be written. The occasion is the central matter or the framing subject in which all portions of the text must be firstly interpreted for the literal meaning. The overall arching theme of St. Paul's First Letter to the Corinthians is to address divisions among the Corinthian faithful that manifest culturally in a variety of ways. The context of the Lord's Supper and the tradition of the institution of the Eucharist found in the writings of St. Paul is driven largely by the social stratification manifesting openly within the conduct of the faithful in the house churches present in Corinth. The reality of the stratification in Corinth can be demonstrated in several passages

---

[8] Wright and Bird, *The New Testament in Its World: An Introduction to the History, Literature, and Theology of the First Christians*, 480.

from St. Paul and St. Luke in which they describe many different roles in Corinthian society that make up the Church. The social roles of Christians are described as city treasurer, ruler of the synagogue, heads of households, benefactors, artisans, merchants, laborers, and slaves.[9]

A Case for the Lord's Supper as Communal Participatory Worship

The analysis of First Corinthians and early Christian worship participating in the Lord's Supper will not cover the entirety of the presented outline. The outline will serve the purpose of showing St. Paul's movement of argument from practical daily living and issues which exist in the Corinthian church, describing many of the cultural divisions which lead up to the manifestation of stratum divisions present during the Lord's Supper. St. Paul begins to pivot toward the Lord's Supper with his concern with the topic of food offered in worship to idols in First Corinthians 8. St. Paul addresses the concern in the community in Corinth about eating food or meat purchased at the market that may have been sacrificed to idols, or eating at a non-Christian home in which the Christian may not know the origins of food.

I. Addressing existing causes of division in Corinth (5:1-6:20)
   a. St. Paul rebukes pagan sexual immorality (5:1-12)

---

[9] Ibid., 482.

b. Legal disputes among the Corinthian faithful (6:1-11)

c. St. Paul's second rebuke of pagan sexual immorality (6:12-20)

II.   Practical Christian living in Corinth (7:1-8:13)
   a. Christian Marriage and Chaste Living (7:1-16)
   b. Christians' function in society (7:17-24)
   c. Addressing the unmarried and widows (7:25-40)
   d. The eating of food offered to pagan gods (8:1-13)

III.   St. Paul's humility for healing divisions (9:1-10:31)
   a. St. Paul yields his rights of an apostle (9:1-24)
   b. Warning the Corinthians against self-confidence (10:1-13)
   c. Warning against the participation in demon worship (10:14-22)
   d. Do all activities for God. (10:23-11:1)

IV.   Participating in the Lord's Supper (11:2-34)
   a. Practical worship: culturally modest and formal dress for worship (11:2-16)
   b. The false Lord's Supper in Corinth (11:17-22)
   c. Instruction of the institution of the Eucharist (11:23-26)
   d. Participating in the Eucharist unworthily (11:27-34)

Biblical commentaries tend to frame and outline St. Paul's discourse for dealing with the community's liturgical difficulties with what Paul refers to as the "Lord's Supper" beginning in chapter 11 verse 2 of First Corinthians.[10] However, Paul begins to set up this issue with the irregular pattern of topics in his rhetoric which is part of a much larger section of passages covering chapters 5:1-16:18.[11] Paul's argument from chapters 5 to 8 deals with daily practical cultural encounters for Christians in Corinth, while chapter 8 begins a hinge-like transition in St. Paul's argument with the concern of idol worship by the practical situation of Christians eating foods or meats offered to idols and later sold in the market. It is here where Paul begins the transition to the topic of proper Christian worship in reference to the Lord's Supper beginning in chapter 8 and moving toward its climax in chapter 11.

Paul's rhetorical form appears to be irregular in his dealing with topics. It is important for the faithful to understand what exactly St. Paul is attempting to convey in Chapter 8, because he addresses the topic of idolatry again in chapter 10, but there is a very important nuance that differs between the two separate thoughts on idolatry. St. Paul's purpose for raising the topic initially is for the Christian community in Corinth to understand the Christian faith is a living, active faith that is lived through its mission given to all Christians by Jesus Christ (Matthew 28:19-20). Pope St. John Paul II explains, "St. Paul reminds the Christians of Corinth of this fact: "For by one Spirit

---

[10] See Introductory notes: *New American Bible*, Revised Edition. (Washington, DC: The United States Conference of Catholic Bishops, 2011), 1 Cor.

[11] Puskas and Reasoner, *The Letters of Paul*, 107.

we are all baptized into one body" (1 Corinthians 12:13), so that the apostle can say to the lay faithful: "Now you are the body of Christ and individually members of it" (1 Corinthians 12:27).[12] The culmination of St. Paul's appeal for Christian unity finds itself in Paul's argument of the baptized becoming members of the body of Christ in chapter 12.

The importance for the current members of the Church is not simply to remain idle but also to be focused on the mission of proclaiming the good news of Jesus Christ to the greater community. So, regarding interreligious difficulties, Paul writes to the Corinthians, "So about the eating of meat sacrificed to idols: we know that 'there is no idol in the world,' and that 'there is no God but one.'"[13] The nuance that St. Paul expresses here is due to the diversity of the Corinthian church containing both Jewish and Gentile Christians. Paul knows from Judaism the strictness of Jewish food laws that would prohibit the eating of food offered to pagan gods; however, these laws would not apply to Gentile converts.[14] For the sake of proclaiming the good news and promoting Christian unity, Paul instructs:

> If someone sees you, with your knowledge, reclining at table
> in the temple of an idol, may not his conscience too, weak as
> it is, be "built up" to eat the meat sacrificed to idols? Thus

---

[12] John Paul II, *Christifideles Laici*, 11. (Vatican City: Libreria Editrice Vaticana, 1988).

[13] 1 Cor. 8:4, NABRE.

[14] Ronald D. Witherup, *Saint Paul and the New Evangelization* (Collegeville: Liturgical Press, 2012), 94.

through your knowledge, the weak person is brought to destruction, the brother for whom Christ died. When you sin in this way against your brothers and wound their consciences, weak as they are, you are sinning against Christ. Therefore, if food causes my brother to sin, I will never eat meat again, so that I may not cause my brother to sin.[15]

The authorial conclusion of St. Paul addressing the discrepancy between various Christians in the Corinth church is for those who are not scandalized by food laws. Although the food laws no longer apply to all Christians, Paul asks the unscandalized to forego any foods having been offered in sacrifice to idols if such knowledge upsets Jewish Christians in the community and causes them to reject the good news of Jesus Christ.

The overall form of this large section of the letter is exhortatory and instructional, but it doesn't seem to follow a linear line of thought. St. Paul appears to break from the topics of daily encounters by meandering in chapter 9 from the topic of worship and sacrificial rituals to becoming concerned with defending his apostolic pedigree. Paul's rhetoric in chapter 9 follows a form referred to as a "Hellenistic diatribe," a judicial form of rhetoric most common in rhetoric schools of the time.[16] It's important to note that Paul is not too concerned with reasserting his authority to the Corinthian church, but rather, Paul wishes to present himself as a model of

---

[15] 1 Cor. 8:10–13, NABRE.

[16] Collins, *First Corinthians*, 333.

humility for the community of Corinth to heal any existing divisions by forgoing what is his by apostolic right:

> Am I not free? Am I not an apostle? Have I not seen Jesus our Lord? Are you not my work in the Lord? [2] Although I may not be an apostle for others, certainly I am for you, for you are the seal of my apostleship in the Lord.[17]

St. Paul first introduces a form of the word apostle with the Greek word ἀπόστολος, distinct from ἀποστολή, which the latter connotes the "office of a special emissary, *apostleship, office of an apostle, assignment.*"[18] In the context of Chapter 9, when it is first introduced, it does not suggest an office or title but rather a function compared to the word "angel/messenger." Paul's use of the word "apostle" in the context of chapter 9 presents himself as a model of humility and unity for the community of the Corinthian church by freely giving up his rights due to the function of his mission in being sent to them.[19] The rhetoric of chapter 9 serves as a pause, which does emphasize St. Paul's authority, but, more importantly, his authority as an apostle "being sent" exists only because the Corinthian church itself exists.[20] Therefore, St. Paul acts as an example of unity for the Corinthians before addressing the concern of idolatry as it

---

[17] 1 Cor. 9:1–2, NABRE.

[18] William Arndt et al., *A Greek-English Lexicon of the New Testament and Other Early Christian Literature* (Chicago: University of Chicago Press, 2000), 121.

[19] Collins, *First Corinthians*, 330.

[20] Witherup, *Saint Paul and the New Evangelization*, 57.

relates to participatory meals of idol worship, which differs greatly from his concern in chapter 8. Fr. Collins further clarifies the distinction, "An idol may be nothing (8:4; 10:19), but participation in such cultic practice can be described as sharing the table of demons."[21]

St. Paul's theology of the Eucharist begins with his juxtaposition of the cup of the Lord and the cup of demons (1 Corinthians 10:14-22). Paul uses the forms of two Greek words, κοινωνός and μετέχω, which the New American Bible translates as "participants" and "partake." The words St. Paul uses carries religious significance to both Christian and pagan cultures which would be present in Corinth. The use of the word "participants" is expressed in the ancient sources as "one who takes part in something with someone."[22] The Greek/English lexicon gives the example in reference to the martyrdom of Polycarp, "Of a martyr (who shares a bloody death w. Christ)."[23] There is great importance for understanding St. Paul's argument against participating in Hellenistic cultic meals that were prevalent in pagan worship for understanding participating in the same single and solitary sacrifice of Jesus:

"The cup of blessing that we bless, is it not a participation in the blood of Christ? The bread that we break, is it not a participation in the body of Christ?"[24]

---

[21] Collins, *First Corinthians*, 376.

[22] Arndt, *A Greek-English Lexicon*, 553.

[23] Ibid, 553.

[24] 1 Cor. 10:16, NABRE.

The word St. Paul uses for participation, κοινωνία, is understood as participation in mutual communion and fellowship with one another.[25] The liturgy of the Eucharist to this day is still referred to as "communion," related to this understanding of participatory worship. Again, the danger for the early Christians in the Corinthian church is that the term in the Greek language was a universal expression of worship in the ancient world.[26] Therefore, one who actively participates in the Hellenistic cult meals celebrated as a pagan rite would be committing the grave sin of idolatry, differing from St. Paul's considerations found in chapter 8 when eating outside of cultic worship practices. Brant Pitre, Michael P. Barber, and John A. Kincaid explain:

> Paul explains that idolatrous meals unite the participants to demons in a way analogous to the Lord's Supper. The parallel is clearer in the Greek: the Lord's Supper involves "participation" or "communion" (*koinōnia*) with Jesus (1 Cor 10:16) just as idolatrous meals make their participants "partners" or "communicants" (*koinōnous*) with demons (1 Cor 10:20).[27]

Note the "partake/participatory" language in St. Paul's warning to the Corinthian church in the final verses of the passage (10:21-

---

[25] Arndt, *A Greek-English Lexicon*, 552.

[26] Collins, *First Corinthians*, 376.

[27] Brant Pitre, Michael P. Barber, and John A. Kincaid, *Paul, a New Covenant Jew: Rethinking Pauline Theology* (Grand Rapids, MI: William B. Eerdmans Publishing Company, 2019), 227.

22). It invokes a connection with the revelation of God's jealousy in the Old Testament canon in comparison to the *kerygma* ("proclamation") of the early Christians:

> You cannot drink the cup of the Lord and also the cup of demons. You cannot partake of the table of the Lord and of the table of demons. Or are we provoking the Lord to jealous anger? Are we stronger than he?[28]

St. Paul, the Misogynist?

The beginning of chapter 11 in First Corinthians again presents more practical daily functions of liturgical worship before getting into the heart of the matter of the Lord's supper. Fr. Collins writes, "For contemporary readers 11:2–16 is one of the most difficult passages in the entire letter."[29] The reason for its difficulty is largely due to the rise of secularism and feminism in Western Christianity. The modern rejection runs so deep that some modern scholars, in reaction to it, have suggested that this portion of the letter is not originally St. Paul because the language and themes differ from St. Paul's other undisputed letters.[30] The arrival in the greater secular culture of gender ideology has thrown into question the definitions of men and women for some. Many clerics and theologians no doubt feel the temptation to redefine over three thousand years of Judeo-Christian anthropology somehow to get with the times. However,

---

[28] 1 Cor. 10:21-22, NABRE.
[29] Collins, *First Corinthians*, 393.
[30] Ibid.

the flow of St. Paul's rhetorical demonstrations throughout his Letter to the Corinthians suggests that the hypothesis that this portion of the letter is not authentically St. Paul is probably wishful thinking. The goal for Bible readers and interpreters is to discover what the living Word of God is attempting to reveal to modern Christianity, considering the authorial context of the passage.

The objection to this passage with the labeling of St. Paul as a misogynist is likely a modern anachronistic interpretation of the text. Modernity is concerned with the topics of feminism, gender, diversity, etc., topics that would not have been at the forefront of issues needing to be addressed in first century Christianity. Some have suggested that the passage may refer to women wearing their hair down while prophesying, which does address some of the overall contexts of the entire letter. Nonetheless, the passage, most likely within the context of the entire letter as it has been discussed, is probably addressing the central issue of social stratum and unity within the liturgy of early Christian worship in Corinth. Furthermore, the context of social stratum continues regarding the practice of the Lord's Supper immediately after this passage.

Abuse of the Lord's Supper at Corinth

The climax of the entire structure of St. Paul's rhetorical argument comes to a head in 1 Corinthians 11:17-34. The *New American Bible Revised Edition* breaks the verses into two separate periscopes. The first addresses the abuse at Corinth, which deals primarily with divisions in the church (verses 17-22). T he second highlights the pre-gospel tradition of the institution of the Eucharist (verses 23-26). Finally, verses 27-34 speak to St. Paul's concern with worthiness in receiving the Eucharist. St. Paul writes to the Corinthians:

> Do you not have houses in which you can eat and drink? Or do you show contempt for the church of God and make those who have nothing feel ashamed? What can I say to you? Shall I praise you? In this matter I do not praise you.[31]

The context for St. Paul's rhetoric here is no doubt caused by the meeting of the more affluent members of the Corinthian church either in secret or prior to the arrival of the working class or slaves. St. Paul exhorts these members of the community, exclaiming to them that their exclusivity in their participatory meals causes a liturgical abuse of disunity, which renders the Lord's Supper void. Maria Pascuzzi explains though, that, "economic disparity is only one aspect of a much larger picture. Established social convention dictated that rank and status be acknowledged by one's place at table and the amount and quality of food and drink one was apportioned."[32] The social norms of culture create division and social stratum, not simply the haves and the have-nots. The issue of social stratum cannot be interpreted through a Marxist dialectic; this would be an anachronistic reading of the issues of Corinth.

---

[31] 1 Cor. 11:22, NABRE.

[32] Maria A. Pascuzzi, "The First Letter to the Corinthians," in *New Testament*, ed. Daniel Durken, The New Collegeville Bible Commentary (Collegeville, MN: Liturgical Press, 2009), 526.

St. Paul moves into the importance of the received tradition of the Lord's Supper, when he says, "For I received from the Lord what I also handed on to you."[33] St. Paul uses the Greek word παραλαμβάνω for "received." The use of the word conveys something very deep in the religious sense. The word in the context ancient Near East tradition means "spiritual heritage… esp. of mysteries and ceremonies that one receives by tradition."[34] St. Paul is stressing to the Corinthian community that these are unique words and of vital importance for the rite and institution of the Lord's Supper in the context of participatory worship of the day. There is a great importance for the authorial audience and today's Catholics and all Christians to understand the origin and tradition of the Eucharist, because it invokes its normative practice in Christianity.[35] The origin recorded in the context of St. Paul's First Letter to the Corinthians of the Lord's Supper, which is the oldest account found in Sacred Scripture, is important for understanding the remarkability of the sacrament of the Eucharist. St. Paul's dialectic demonstration of comparting and contrasting Hellenistic participatory worship and pagan participatory worship with the proper understanding of the rite of the Lord's Supper no doubt establishes the foundation for the commemoration of the Mass as understood in present-day Catholicism. St. Paul, and St. Luke in his account, establishes a firm understanding that the formula to which St. Paul refers in 11:23-26

---

[33] 1 Cor. 11:23, NABRE.
[34] Arndt, *A Greek-English Lexicon*, 768.
[35] Collins, *First Corinthians*, 425.

indicates a tradition and liturgical form that had been actively used since the earliest days of Christianity.

Reflection: A Place for Sinners and Participating in the Eucharist Unworthily

There has been much ink spilled in contemporary Catholic theology on the topic of the unworthiness of receiving the Eucharist, especially as it pertains to Catholic politicians who reject longstanding Catholic moral theology. It is fitting to end this chapter with an exegetical interpretation of 1 Corinthians 11:27:34 for the everyday Catholic. For St. Paul, Bible readers might ask, what does "discerning" and "unworthiness" mean to St. Paul and to the Corinthians? The purpose of this reflection is not to retread an analysis of what has already been extensively written on the topic of Catholics who may find themselves in a state of mortal sin and are compelled to seek out the Sacrament of Confession before receiving Jesus Christ in the Eucharist. Nonetheless, there is tension within the Catholic understanding of the purpose of the Eucharist and who can receive, especially in the development of the doctrine during the Scholastic period of the Church. Bishop Robert Barron explains this tension:

> The Eucharistic meal is the place where sinners are especially welcome, for it is the place where they will find precisely what they need. Why then, we might wonder, does Thomas contend that the Eucharist ought not to be received by someone in the state of Mortal Sin? By definition, mortal sin is a wrong that has so radically compromised one's relation to

God that it has effectively killed the divine life in the one who commits it. Therefore, just as it would be foolish to give medicine to a dead person, it would be counterindicated, Thomas concludes, to offer the healing power of the Eucharist to one who is spiritually dead.[36]

So, naturally, this begs the question: those who commit mortal sin and have not confessed—who are they? And, more importantly, how can the Church, in its mission of preaching the gospel, reach them with the good news of the forgiveness of sins and eternal life? Pope Francis enlightens the faithful about the purpose of the Eucharist which shares in the missionary aspect of the Church in *Evangelii Gaudium*:

> The Eucharist, although it is the fullness of sacramental life, is not a prize for the perfect but a powerful medicine and nourishment for the weak. These convictions have pastoral consequences that we are called to consider with prudence and boldness. Frequently, we act as arbiters of grace rather than its facilitators. But the Church is not a tollhouse; it is the house of the Father, where there is a place for everyone, with all their problems.[37]

---

[36] Robert Barron, *Eucharist* (Park Ridge: Word on Fire Institute, 2021), 98.

[37] Pope Francis, *Evangelii Gaudium*, Apostolic Exhortation (Vatican City: Libreria Editrice Vaticana, 2013), 40-41.

Therefore, there must be for the proclaimer of the gospel of Jesus Christ an understanding of the missionary purpose of the Church, which always finds itself antithetical to existing divisions in the Church, which is the literal context for the occasion of St. Paul's First Letter to the Corinthians. Of course, it is important not to misconstrue this notion with Jesus' teaching that He is the cause of division between those who choose to follow Him and the world (Luke 12:49-53). The context is different between the two passages. The example of Jesus expresses a choice between the love of God or the love of the world. St. Paul's occasion for writing a letter to the Corinthians is an expression toward a community of believers of the new covenant of Jesus Christ.

There are some Catholics who seek out and condemn other groups of Catholics who may rightly be concerned with the form of liturgy and devotional practices. These Catholics often refer to these groups as "rigid," but it's important to reflect on St. Paul's example to the entirety of the Body of Christ found in the Church of Corinth—Paul does not address groups or factions but addresses issues. Paul understands the nuances of religious expression, which may cause some groups to be scandalized; he doesn't fan the fire by supporting these religious expressions, but implores those who find no scandal in them to refrain from such actions when necessary. St. Paul may address the rigidity of food laws; however, he does not promote the opposite of rigidness, which is instability for the church of Corinth. In both chapters 10 and 11, on matters of high doctrinal importance, Paul's teaching on idolatry, unity, and discernment provides clarity to the Corinthian church, instead of creating any sort of confusion among believers.

Pope Francis imparts the importance of unity when it comes to the Lord's Supper among the Christian faithful when writing: "We cannot break bread on Sunday if our hearts are closed to our brothers and sisters. We cannot partake of that Bread if we do not give bread to the hungry. We cannot share that Bread unless we share the sufferings of our brothers and sisters in need."[38]

The fact on the ground regarding the Catholic Church is that Catholics find themselves divided on many issues in the Church. The interpretation of St. Paul's text here is not meant to enumerate the issues and solve them. The purpose, hopefully, is a recognition of the need of cultivating the virtues of humility and charity. Disagreements and debate do not necessarily mean disunity among us. Every Catholic and every Christian should strive in our debates with our fellow Christians to cultivate the virtues of humility and charity in the hope that by coming together to discuss such ideas, we can revitalize the faith and proclaim the saving power of Jesus Christ, united with each other by discovering the truth in God's revelation.

---

[38] Pope Francis, Twitter Post, June 7, 2021, 6:30 AM. Online at https://twitter.com/Pontifex/status/1401864013458280458.

Chapter 4

Jesus, the Bridegroom of the Soul

John Tuttle

I put before you the one great thing to love on earth: the Blessed Sacrament. There you will find romance, glory, honour, fidelity, and the true way of all your loves upon earth, and more than that: Death: by the divine paradox, that which ends life, and demands the surrender of all, and yet by the taste (or foretaste) of which alone can what you seek in your earthly relationships (love, faithfulness, joy) be maintained, or take on that complexion of reality, of eternal endurance, which every man's heart desires. – J.R.R. Tolkien[1]

Our Catholic faith does a terrific job with acknowledging that which is beautiful. We see this reality reflected in our churches, in the lives of the saints, and in the very essence of the Mass. After all, God Himself is the infinite, inexhaustible Beauty from Whom all blessings and beauties flow.

The faith in which we partake is a growing relationship with the living God. This connection of love—of God giving Himself to us and inviting us to give of ourselves in return—is also beautiful. Our

---

1 Humphrey Carpenter, ed., *The Letters of J.R.R. Tolkien* (New York, NY: Houghton Mifflin Company, 2000), 53-54.

relationship with God transcends and informs our relationships with everyone around us.

In an age where in-person socializing is declining, along with Catholics' belief in the real Presence of God the Son in the Holy Eucharist, it seems a return to the fundamentals of Christianity is overdue. Less than a third of U.S. Catholics believe that the altar bread and wine literally become the Body, Blood, Soul, and Divinity of our Lord Jesus.[2]

This fact should be alarming. The Most Blessed Sacrament is what gives vitality to the Catholic Church. The very Body of Christ feeds the members of His mystical body; the very Blood of Christ pulses through the veins of that same mystical body, pouring out over each of us, marking us as children of God and washing us of our sins.

Simultaneously, American culture is currently witnessing a decrease in marriages. According to a 2019 survey, only 53 percent of the U.S. populace that's old enough to get married has done so, which is a comparable deficiency from decades past.[3]

Perhaps the drop in belief in Jesus' Presence in the Eucharist and the decline in finding a calling to matrimony are purely coincidental. However, it might belie a deeper problem in our society: that we

---

2 Gregory A. Smith, "Just one-third of U.S. Catholics agree with their church that Eucharist is body, blood of Christ," Pew Research. Online at https://www.pewresearch.org/fact-tank/2019/08/05/transubstantiation-eucharist-u-s-catholics/.

3 Juliana Menasce Horowitz, Nikki Graf, and Gretchen Livingston, "Marriage and Cohabitation in the U.S," Pew Research. Online at https://pewresearch.org/social-trends/2019/11/06/marriage-and-cohabitation-in-the-u-s/.

have forgotten how to love. In a world where cozy comforts tend to dominate our thoughts and actions, the longevity and fidelity toward one's vocation, a genuine yet rigorous relationship, have become increasingly rarer to find in our culture.

It would seem that the Holy Eucharist and family life—the offshoot of marriage—go hand-in-hand. Indeed, they are both callings to love, although in different circumstances and in varying degrees. Nevertheless, the similarity of Holy Communion and holy matrimony, and the shared theological imagery they have in common, help us understand the Eucharist as a communion with a Person, an intimate relationship that we ought to desire. At the same time, we see how Christ's example of love shows us how spouses ought to love one another.

The one sacrament can help us better understand the other, and vice versa. Each, as God designed, invites us into a deeper rhythm of love, of opening ourself up to the other, of being receptive to the other's love, and of giving our own.

Is There Such a Thing as Love?

We look around at the world at large, and we can certainly say there are terrible things happening. Evil is a reality that must be faced. But focusing predominantly on the ills of our society makes for an unsettled heart and a mind fixed on visible evils instead of the intrinsic good God has bestowed on His creation and which He continues to provide.

Still, the images of numerous sins and atrocities stand out and can make us wonder if there even is such a thing as love. In response, I would have to say there *is*, in fact, love on display in the people around us. If we seek it out, we can see what true love looks like. Look back on the weighty date of September 11, 2001. An act of terrorism assaulted not only monuments, but also tore apart families. Yet we also witnessed the stunning sacrifice of many firemen and first responders and, in its aftermath, the charity of numerous men and women.

The Nazi concentration camps of World War II exemplify another horror that was all too real. Any of the 7,000 prisoners who were liberated from Auschwitz in 1945 could attest to the authenticity of such places of tragic repute. Invasive experiments, starvation and laborious work, and myriad ways of murder were their business. Yet, out of unspeakable cruelty, stood saints like Maximilian Kolbe, a Franciscan priest who offered his life for a man he didn't even know. A concentration camp became the hallowed ground on which a martyr received his coronation.

Under ancient Roman rule, crucifixion was a uniquely humiliating and painful method of execution. More than that, as with much of Rome's brutality, it was a spectacle. There are accounts of mass crucifixions, events in which perhaps hundreds were systematically crucified. The so-called *Pax Romana* was like a hilltop utopia with mangled corpses and crosses paving the way. This was not the peace that Jesus Christ promised. Rather, He offers true peace, a way of life beyond what the world desires and revels in. Jesus became the victim of the world's raging evil. In Christ's crucifixion, we see our sin overthrown and Love incarnate pouring Himself out.

Our Lord says, "Greater love has no one than this, that someone lay down his life for his friends."[4] And Jesus lived that love. Christ's crucifixion is an act of love that's outrageous; it's also noble. That which was the most unjust thing imaginable, putting God to death, has become our justification.

At the end of the day, what is love? Hopefully, the foregoing examples have directed us to the right answer: it is seeking another's good despite what one suffers to attain it. This love is a selfless activity. Both the Holy Eucharist and holy matrimony call us into this kind of relationship.

The Eucharist as a Marriage-Like Union

The context in which Jesus presents Himself before His apostles in the Holy Eucharist is telling. It happens at the meeting we now famously dub the "Last Supper." But it was so much more than just a meal. Consider that the blunt fact that He would be tried and killed in a matter of hours was ever on Jesus's mind. Yet, He does not trouble about Himself. Rather, He thinks of His beloved: the apostles, the first forerunners of the gospel, the seeds of the Church. Jesus provides them with the Sacrament of Divine Love, a self-giving which leaves Himself vulnerable. The apostles can receive Him in this Communion in faith—as many presumably did—or they could be like Judas and receive this enormous Gift in sin, with indifference and disinterest. We know Judas spurned the real Presence in the

---

[4] John 15:13.

Eucharist because he spurned Jesus in the garden, betraying Him to death. Denying the Eucharist is a rejection of Jesus.

The Eucharist, like marriage, is a union between two persons. It is an intimate and mysterious relationship, just as marriage is intimate and mysterious to varying degrees. To get a handle on what we mean by the Eucharist inviting us into a marriage-like communion, let's revisit what marriage is and what kind of relationship with God we are called to.

As presented in the Genesis narrative, marriage is the first interpersonal relationship shared between two human beings and, by necessity, it's also the foundation of social *community*, of communicating and living together. The Bible describes the marital union as an action both tangible and intimate, so intimate that whereas there had been two persons prior to marriage, afterward there is only one. Genesis 2:24 says, "Therefore a man leaves his father and mother and *cleaves to his wife*, and they become one flesh."

Human beings are body-soul composites. Our life, our being, is tied up in our existence as having both a body and a soul, fused together, which are but one entity. Hence, when scripture speaks of man and woman becoming one flesh, they also become one in spirit. To this day, marriage is upheld as a sacred act in which the two are joined together as one.

Note the verb *cleave* that is used in the passage above. This word choice is vivid but not shocking, since marriage is meant to include a physical connection between spouses. Interestingly, in later verses, the Bible uses similar language in how we ought to aspire to a deep, close relationship with God. For instance:

You shall walk after the LORD your God and fear him, and keep his commandments and obey his voice, and you shall serve him and *cleave to him.*[5]

This description seems to align with the relationship Adam and Eve enjoyed with God in Paradise prior to their direct disobedience in which they did not heed the voice of God, nor obey Him. When we imagine ourselves walking with God, we are like children; we clutch at His hand or hold tight to part of the Master's garment. But our first parents abandoned this. They let go of God and clung instead to something which was a delight to the eyes, something that smacked of a surge in personal power, something that promised a better reality that ultimately fell short.

However, in Deuteronomy, as in Genesis before, we are presented with the idea of a human person clinging or cleaving to another person. Genesis speaks of the man and woman cleaving together. The verse from Deuteronomy directs us to another calling, to an even taller order of coming into intimate contact with a divine Person. God invites us, like the Prodigal Son, like a repentant child, to run back to His embrace.

There are many more of these examples from scripture, ones that employ imagery that's much more specific to the marital covenant. In the book of Isaiah, for example, the prophet compares God to a joyful bridegroom and the people of Israel to an unfaithful wife to whom God nevertheless bestows mercy. Significantly, Jesus calls *Himself* the Bridegroom, a connection that announces both His

---

[5] Deuteronomy 13:4.

divine nature and the type of relationship He extends to His follow-ers.[6]

This gives us an idea of the intimacy God longs to have with each of us. Throughout the Old and New Testaments, God communi-cates His love for His people through marital language, a language of deep and abiding love. As the *Catechism of the Catholic Church* tells us, "The entire Christian life bears the mark of the spousal love of Christ and the Church."[7]

St. Paul can further back up this statement with his inspired writ-ings. In short, the love of Jesus Christ, the relationship with this Most Holy Person, is comparable to marriage. It is the wedding of the human and the divine, a mystery that Jesus—being the *first-born of all creation* that *in everything he might be pre-eminent*[8]—first ac-tualizes through the Incarnation. Thereafter, via the institution of the Holy Eucharist, we too are permitted to join in this reality in a unique way: the wedding of our fallen humanity with the splendid divinity of Christ.

In matrimony (the union of a man and a woman), the difference between the two sexes displays an *otherness* that is at once as much of a contrast as it is a complementarity. Similarly, in Holy Commu-nion, our human nature is met with Someone entirely *other*, entirely transcendent, entirely above and beyond our limited faculties. In Communion, we touch the divine Jesus, and He touches us. In

---

6 See Matthew 9:15; Mark 2:19-20; Luke 5:34-35. In addition to Jesus Himself, John the Baptist and other prophets refer to Him as "bride-groom."

7 CCC 1617.

8 See Colossians 1:15-20.

receiving the Eucharist, I oftentimes find the Sacred Host *cleaving* to my tongue or the roof of my mouth. And it's here that the human and divine, by nature wholly different, are reconciled, united, and complimented, even as they are in Jesus Himself. Here the Christian becomes truly Christian because he enters physically and spiritually into the life of Jesus Christ.

Speaking as a disciple to his Lord, Thomas à Kempis writes about this interpersonal Communion in *The Imitation of Christ*:

> O happy mind and blessed soul which deserves to receive You, her Lord God, and in receiving You, is filled with spiritual joy! How great a Master she entertains, what a beloved guest she receives, how sweet a companion she welcomes, how true a friend she gains, how beautiful and noble is the spouse she embraces, beloved and desired above all things that can be loved and desired![9]

À Kempis talks about receiving the Eucharistic Lord as a spouse. The soul is here considered feminine, thus signifying the soul's need to be receptive to the love of another. Once again, here in the Catholic tradition, as in scripture itself, the Lord Jesus is understood in the context of being the Bridegroom. In the Gospels, He is the Bridegroom of His disciples—the spouse of His Church. And if the Church is made up of many individuals, just as the body consists of many parts, then Jesus is also the spouse of our souls.

---

9 Thomas à Kempis, *The Imitation of Christ* (Milwaukee, WI: The Bruce Publishing Company, 1940), 222.

If we look closely at the scripture passages noted earlier, we notice that God extends His love to us while we are still sinners. Adam and Eve abandoned His embrace; the Israelites have been like an unfaithful spouse. Yet, God is merciful, and His love isn't going anywhere. It is easy then, and perhaps in some ways beneficial, to consider the severity of our sin and our total dependency on Jesus' mercy and saving action in a romantic context. Jesus is always extending His love to us. We, who continually lapse back into sin, are asked by God to love Him in return. An eloquent poem that I believe captures these sentiments of passion and penitence quite well is "Batter My Heart" by John Donne. There the poet writes:

Bitter my heart, three-personed God; for you
As yet but knock, breathe, shine and seek to mend.
That I may rise and stand, o'erthrow me and bend
Your force to break, blow, burn and make me new.
I, like an usurped town, to another due,
Labor to admit you, but, oh, to no end;
Reason, your viceroy in me, me should defend,
But is captived and proves weak or untrue.
Yet dearly I love you and would be loved fain,
But am betrothed unto your enemy:
Divorce me, untie or break the knot again,
Take me to you, imprison me, for I,
Except you enthrall me, never shall be free,

Nor ever chaste, except you ravish me.[10]

This poem seems to come from a deep place of sorrow and desperation of prayer. The writer, like any of us, struggles with sin and falls back into it time and again. He owns up to his deficiency, his total dependence on God. Sinfulness puts us in league with the devil (being "betrothed unto your enemy"). But Jesus still extends His forgiveness and intimacy to us, particularly in the Eucharist, where—if only tarnished by venial sins—I can become spiritually *chaste*, washed of those sins, in this sacrament where my Lord *ravishes me*.

As infinite as God is, the beauties of the Holy Eucharist are never-ending. Let's turn now to the needs of marriage and how matrimony points us to the respect we must show for Jesus, the Spouse of our souls!

What Marriage Is and What It Means for Our Relationship with Jesus

As ordained by the Creator, and consecrated to the position of sacrament by God the Son, marriage is the official joining of a man and a woman. As Genesis states, this union is exhibited by the man cleaving to his wife. Note that it says "wife," not "wives." Christian (that is, sacramental) marriage is a monogamous and exclusive relationship involving just one man and one woman. It's this kind of exclusivity that God desires for us to have when it comes to worship and religious reverence. Embedded at the outset of the Ten

---

10 Louis Untermeyer, ed., *The Book of Living Verse* (New York, NY: Harcourt, Brace and Company, 1945), 86-87.

Commandments is the decree, "You shall have no other gods before me" (Deuteronomy 5:7).

This means we don't worship angels or demons or men or any other creatures simply on the basis of what they are—*created* beings—as opposed to the Creator: God Who is pure Being and through Whom all things were made. The Creator of all is the One deserving my reverence and my worship. (On another level, "other gods" could be mere things to which we devote too much time, desire, or attention.) Despite God's inaugural commandment, it seemed to be the one the Hebrews neglected most frequently. Idolatry spread up repeatedly through Israel's history, provoking from God such labels as *harlot* and *unfaithful spouse* for His chosen people.

We don't want to fall into similar trouble. Thus, God calls us to an exclusive relationship with Himself, not one with the world and its enticements. We must turn continually from created things to the Creator Who sustains and helps His creation. The liturgy, the climactic point of which is the Eucharist, is the highest form of human worship, since it was initiated by Christ and has been shaped by the Holy Spirit. Receiving the Holy Eucharist at Mass is the consummation of our relationship with the divine. Just as the conjugal act in marriage is the consummation of a physical and spiritual relationship between spouses, Holy Communion is a consummation of our relationship with God, a moment in which God's presence is experienced physically as well as spiritually. And this reception can make our souls perfect, spotless in the eyes of God.

When a man and woman desire to enter into the sexual act in a way that is condoned by God, our faith informs us of a few ground rules. First, the two must be married; they must already be united in the spousal relationship. Second, each party must understand that their spouse is not a thing, not an object, but a *person*. Our relationship with Jesus in the Eucharist has similar prerequisites.

First, we must be in an active and living relationship with God; we must be baptized and be living in a state of grace (that is, not living in mortal sin). Second, we must understand that when we receive the Host, we receive not a thing, but a *Person*. This here is no longer bread. Through Jesus' words, it became the Body of Christ at the consecration during Mass. And just as the conjugal embrace is considered sacred within marriage, so too Communion with God is sacred.

The conjugal act between spouses is generally seen as an integral part of marriage, the element by which new life is made possible. Likewise, Jesus Himself emphasizes the importance of Holy Communion: "Unless you eat the flesh of the Son of man and drink his blood, you have no life in you" (John 6:53).

Furthermore, each act of intercourse within marriage has the potential to strengthen the bond between husband and wife. This is also part of what receiving the Holy Eucharist is intended to do. Our faith in God is like any other relationship; it can either grow stronger or start to flounder. The more Communions we receive in a state of grace, the better our relationship with God can become. Life is a progressive journey, and Jesus offers Himself as the sustenance for that journey. Every Communion can help us grow closer to God, benefit from more graces, and do better in approaching our lives with a focus on charity and selflessness.

As beautiful as these aspects of the sacraments are, marriage does not stop at sex, nor Christianity at Holy Communion. Our Christian lifestyle must take the graces from these holy interactions and let them overflow into every dimension of our lives. The building up of these relationships—through intercourse and in Holy Communion—helps us live righteously according to the life and graces God has given us. With each Communion as with each conjugal act, the practicing Catholic and the faithful spouse are called to deeper self-sacrifice. We're called to an ever-deepening love, a love that reaches outside of oneself to serve others.

We've just seen how the context of marriage can help us better understand the divine Person of Jesus Christ in the Eucharist. Let's now look at how Christ's example as the Bridegroom should influence the lifestyle and decisions made by spouses within the sacrament of marriage.

Marriage as a Christ-Like Vocation of Denying Oneself

We've already discussed the institution of the Holy Eucharist and the beauty that shines forth from this Most Blessed Sacrament. But what of Christ's passionate love? Yes, we know He gives Himself to us. This is a sign of love. But our fallen human nature is always seeking, always wanting, always in need, always questioning. Jesus responded by emptying Himself. So where do we see His love for us? It is seen in His agonies, His sufferings, His longings. And His longings are for us. He *thirsts* for us, for our wellbeing, and for our unity with Him.

Jesus, as Bridegroom to the Church, shows by His sacrifice what spousal love looks like in its perfection. Desire for union with one's spouse is meant to be coupled with a desire for her entire wellbeing, particularly for the spouse's soul. Simply put, God wants spouses to learn to love each other the way God loves them.

In word and deed, Jesus Christ shows us how best to do this since He is God and thus, as St. Paul points out, He commits no sin.[11] In his writings, Paul addresses marriage on several occasions, perhaps none as bluntly and potently as in the letter to the Ephesians. There he not only goes over what spouses must do for one another and their families, but he also compares spousal love to the love Christ has shown us.

"Therefore be imitators of God, as beloved children," the Apostle tells us. "And walk in love, as Christ loved us and gave himself up for us, a fragrant offering and sacrifice to God" (Ephesians 5:1-2). When it comes to those who are married, Paul gets more specific with *how* we imitate God the Son:

> Wives, be subject to your husbands, as to the Lord. For the husband is the head of the wife as Christ is the head of the church, his body, and is himself its Savior. (Ephesian 5:22-23)

As part of the Church, we are all called to be like wives in the sense that we must submit ourselves to God in humility. But within the family, Paul here reminds wives they are to "be subject" to their

---

11 See 2 Corinthians 5:21.

husbands, which emphasizes a need for humility and docility within marriage. The inspired writer goes on:

> Husbands, love your wives, as Christ loved the church and gave himself up for her, that he might sanctify her, having cleansed her by the washing of water with the word.... Even so husbands should love their wives as their own bodies. He who loves his wife loves himself. For no man ever hates his own flesh, but nourishes and cherishes it, as Christ does the church, because we are members of his body. (Ephesians 5:25, 26, 28-30)

This latter half of Paul's address to spouses illustrates the expectations a husband is called to live up to. Like Jesus, he must love his beloved to the point that he's willing to *give himself up for her*, to die for her if necessary. As Christ lovingly watches over His Church, so God invites husbands to love their wives with tenderness and care, to ever be on the lookout for their perfection, particularly spiritual perfection, just as Christ washed His bride of her sinful stains.

The Pauline passage from above alludes to the subtle sameness of each spouse's calling, a complimentary sameness in the differences. A continual willingness for the wife to subject herself to the husband's will is an act of self-denial. In turn, the husband must be worthy of this trust his wife places in him. His vocation involves, like the wife's, daily self-denial. He must put his own feelings, desires, and what may seem to be *needs* aside in order to make his wife and her growth in virtue and health his new priorities. Both spouses must die to themselves, denying themselves for the sake of the other.

Paul gives us a picture of this self-sacrifice, an example to live up to, in the Person of Jesus. This selflessness is at the heart of genuine love. If we want to learn this self-sacrificial love, we should turn to this same Person. It is Jesus in the Eucharist!

You'll notice I included a terrific quote from the Catholic author J.R.R. Tolkien at the beginning of this chapter. It is a beautiful tribute to the sacrament in which Jesus offers us nothing short of Himself. In the adoration and reception of Him there, we may still find romance and the purification of all our loves in this life.

If we approach Him with honest hearts, He can and will instill faith and charity within us. If we desire to live as just people in our country, if we wish to have more marriages marked by fidelity and felicity, let's turn to Jesus to show us how. If we wish to marry, let us first love the Spouse of our souls. If married, let us taste and see the goodness of Jesus and of His love, in order that we may love others better. Tolkien knew Who he was talking about. Whatever state of life we find ourselves in along our earthly journey, it's the Holy Eucharist, the Person of Jesus Christ, through Whom we can eventually attain that "which every man's heart desires."

Chapter 5

The Real Presence of Christ in the Eucharist

Christina M. Sorrentino

"God dwells in our midst, in the Blessed Sacrament of the altar." -St. Maximilian Kolbe

The Catholic Church uses the theological term "Real Presence" to mean that Christ is physically present in the Eucharist in the form of simple bread and wine that has been transubstantiated by the power of the Holy Spirit into the actual and literal Body and Blood of Jesus Christ.[1] Transubstantiation, the greatest treasure and mystery of the Catholic Church, is the miracle that occurs daily upon the altar during every single Catholic Mass. The term "transubstantiation" is derived from the two Latin words, *trans* meaning "across," as in change or movement, and *substantia* meaning "substance," and it seems to have first begun being discussed as early as the mid-300's as stated by St. Cyril of Jerusalem in his mystagogical lectures:

> Do not think of the elements as bare bread and wine; they are, according to the Lord's declaration, the Body and Blood of Christ. Though sense suggests the contrary, let faith be your stay. Instead of judging the matter by taste, let faith give

---

[1]See *Catechism of the Catholic Church*, 2nd ed. (Washington DC: United States Catholic Conference, 2011), 1333, 1353, 1357.

you an unwavering confidence that you have been privileged
to receive the Body and Blood of Christ.[2]

The term was first used by Hildebert of Tours, in 1079 depicting
what was happening to the bread and wine during the Holy Sacrifice
of the Mass.[3]

In the early Church the belief in transubstantiation was not re-
futed by Christians. The well-known and very respected Protestant
scholar J.N.D. Kelly wrote: "Eucharistic teaching, it should be understood at the outset, was in general unquestioningly realist, i.e. the
consecrated bread and wine were taken to be, and were treated and
designated as, the Savior's body and blood."[4] The Oxford scholar
Darwell Stone backs up Kelly's statement: "Throughout the writings
of the Fathers there is unbroken agreement that the consecrated
bread and wine are the Body and Blood of Christ, and that the Eucharist is a sacrifice."[5] The Fathers of the Church together did not
deny the Real Presence of Jesus in the Eucharist.

Transubstantiation is when there is a substantial conversion
where the whole substance of the bread and the whole substance of
the wine are changed into the Body, Blood, Soul, and Divinity of

---

[2] Cyril of Jerusalem, *Mystagogical Lectures: Fourth Lecture on the Mysteries*, 6.

[3] "The Real Presence of Christ in the Eucharist," *Catholic Encyclopedia*,
(1909). Online at https://www.newadvent.org/cathen/ 05573a.htm

[4] J.N.D. Kelly, *Early Christian Doctrines* (New York: Harper & Row,
1960), 440.

[5] Darwell Stone, *The Holy Communion*, from the Oxford Library of
Practical Theology, (South Yarra Victoria, Australia: Leopold Publishing,
2016), 37.

Jesus Christ; True God, and true man as He sits at the right hand of God the Father in heaven. The whole Christ is truly, really, and substantially made present in each species; only the accidents of the bread and the wine remain at the moment of consecration. The *terminus formalis a quo* (substance of bread and wine) no longer exists and there commences the Real Presence of Christ; the beginning of the *terminus formalis ad quem* (Christ's Body and Blood).[6] Fr. James T. O'Connor, a highly regarded authority on dogmatic and sacramental theology wrote:

> The mystery of Transubstantiation is a totally marvelous change but not one wherein the Lord descends from heavenly glory to "enter" under the appearances of bread and wine. Rather it is one in which he, not coming down, lifts the creaturely realities to himself, drawing them up to where he is now with the Father. He draws them to himself in such a fashion that he subjugates them and so transforms their own being that it becomes identical with his. The very being of bread and wine is lifted out of itself in a mighty spiral of ascent, is subsumed by and converted into the reality of Jesus seated in glory. By drawing the reality of all the elements scattered throughout the world unto and into himself, Jesus maintains his own bodily unity. The elements are changed into him, not he into them. If he did to the appearances, the species, what he does to the very reality of the bread and

---

[6] See CCC 1375-1377; Dr. Ludwig Ott, *Fundamentals of Catholic Dogma* (Rockford, IL: The Mercier Press, 1960), 380.

wine, then, once the Consecration of the Mass was finished, the priest would be left with nothing before him on the paten or in the cup, and Christ would appear in glory. For then not only the being but the very appearances that manifest that being to the world would have been submitted into the exalted Lord, and human history on earth would have reached its conclusion.[7]

We take part in the heavenly liturgy where our intimate encounter with Christ is mediated to the Church through earthly bread and wine, that which has been revealed to us to be where His Real Presence is found. The liturgical celebration of the Eucharist is a means of "turning around of exitus to reditus, of departure to return, of God's descent to our assent".[8] It was the climax of the exitus when the Son of God being sent by the Father descended from heaven to take on human flesh at the Incarnation; the revelation of the Second Person of the Trinity, bringing humanity into union with God. Our reditus is when we respond to the Incarnation, the Crucifixion, and the Resurrection. It is our return to God when we receive and consume the Eucharist, having a sacramental encounter with Christ that purifies, illumines, and perfects us, when our reality ascends to heaven drawing us back to unity and perfect harmony with God.[9]

---

[7] Fr. James T. O'Connor, *The Hidden Manna: A Theology of the Eucharist,* 2nd Ed. (San Francisco, CA: Ignatius Press, 1988), 291-292.

[8] Joseph Ratzinger, *The Spirit of Liturgy: Commemorative Edition*, (San Francisco: Ignatius Press, 2018), 75.

[9] Fr. Phillip Michael Tangorra, *Holiness and Living the Sacramental Life* (Ohio: Emmaus Road, 2017), 18-19, 148.

The Church teaches that the Body and Blood united with the Soul and Divinity of Christ, the whole Person of Jesus Christ, is real, true, and present in the most Blessed Sacrament of the Eucharist.[10] The human person is formed through the sacrament of Baptism in the "image and likeness" of God,[11] corporeal and spiritual, having a body and soul,[12] therefore the Son of Man has His whole human nature together with His whole Divine nature in the Eucharist. The humanity of Christ is hypostatically united with His Divinity; He is consubstantial with the Father and the Holy Spirit.[13] As True God and true man He is fully present in the Eucharist as the Second Person of the Blessed Trinity.[14]

It is not optional for Catholics to believe in transubstantiation; it is an article of faith[15] that at the consecration, the substance of the bread and the wine undergo a conversion into the Body and Blood of Christ, and Christ becomes really and truly present in the

---

[10] See Thomas Aquinas, Summa Theologiae III, q. 76. a. 1-4; Pope Paul VI, *Sacrosanctum Concilium*, 47. Online at https://www.vatican.va/; Pope John Paul II, Encyclical *Ecclesia de Eucharistia, 15-16: AAS 95 (2003)*. Online at https://www.vatican.va/; See *CCC 1381.*

[11] See Second Vatican Council, Dogmatic Constitution of the Church, *Lumen Gentium*, 6: AAS 57 (1965). Online at https://www.vatican.va/

[12] See *CCC 362-368.*

[13] Dr. Ludwig Ott, *Fundamentals of Catholic Dogma* (Rockford, IL: The Mercier Press, 1960), 384.

[14] Fr. Phillip Michael Tangorra, *Holiness and Living the Sacramental Life* (Ohio: Emmaus Road, 2017), 101.

[15] Fr. Benedict J. Groeschel, and James Monti, *In the Presence of Our Lord: The History, Theology, and Psychology of Eucharistic Devotion* (Huntington, IA: Our Sunday Visitor Publishing, 1997), 55.

Eucharist. St. Thomas Aquinas brings attention to the fact that in Sacred Scripture Christ at the Last Supper is not quoted saying the words, "This bread is my body," but, "This is my body."[16] The consecration of the Eucharist takes place at the "words of institution"[17] spoken by the priest, *in persona Christi Capitis,* which effects the Sacrament, and had been declared by the Council of Florence as an official position of the Magisterium.[18]

When the words, "Body of Christ," are heard moments before receiving Holy Communion it is important to look beyond the visible "bread" that can be seen by eyes alone, and to reflect upon what it has become by Christ's words, and the epiclesis, the invocation of the Holy Spirit; the Body of Christ.[19] When the communicant responds with "Amen," he is giving an affirmation of his profession of faith in the Real Presence of Jesus in the Eucharist.[20] Transubstantiation was adopted as a significant expression by the ecumenical councils of The Fourth Council of the Lateran (1215), and the Council of Lyons (1274) in the Greek Emperor Michael Palaeologus' pro-

---

[16] ST III, q. 78. a. 5.

[17] *The Daily Roman Missal,* "Eucharistic Prayer I (Roman Canon)" (Woodbridge, IL: Rev. James Socias, 1993-2012), "Eucharistic Prayer I (Roman Canon)," 775.

[18] See Ecumenical Council of Florence, Session VIII, 22 November 1439, [Bull of Union with the Armenians]: DS 1314. Online at https://www.papalencyclicals.net/councils/ecum17.htm

[19] See St. Irenaeus, *Against Heresies,* IV.16.28.

[20] *The Mystery of the Eucharist in the Life of the Church* (Washington, DC: United States Conference of Catholic Bishops, 2021), No. 22, 14-15.

fession of faith.[21] It was then dogmatically defined and summarized in the following statement of the Council of Trent:

> Because Christ our Redeemer said that it was truly his body that he was offering under the species of bread, it has always been the conviction of the Church of God, and this holy Council now declares again, that by the consecration of the bread and wine there takes place a change of the whole substance of the bread into the substance of the body of Christ our Lord and of the whole substance of the wine into the substance of his blood. This change the holy Catholic Church has fittingly and properly called transubstantiation.[22]

The Church focuses on the reality of Christ's Flesh and Blood present in the Eucharist, and not the earthly realities of the bread and wine. The reality is that Christ is not simply spiritually present, but is actually present physically to provide us with True Food and True Drink, as the sacrificial victim and sacrificial priest. Fr. John A. Hardon in his commentary on the Real Presence states:

> We might then say that the Eucharistic Presence of Christ is at once a reality and a relationship. It is a reality because Christ really is in the Eucharist. So that the Real Presence of

---

[21] "The Real Presence of Christ in the Eucharist," *Catholic Encyclopedia*, (1909). Online at https://www.newadvent.org/cathen/05573a.htm

[22] Ecumenical Council of Trent, Session XIII, 11 October 1551, Decree on the Most Holy Eucharist, Chapter 4: DS 1642. Online at https://www.papalencyclicals.net/councils/trent.htm; CCC 1376.

Christ postulates on faith the real absence of bread and wine. He *is* now where before the consecration *were* bread and wine. They are gone and He is there. What before was real bread and wine is now only the external properties of bread and wine. He is here in the Eucharist truly present. They are no longer present but only their species or, as we say, appearances.[23]

It is in the Eucharist that the whole Christ is contained; Body, Blood, Soul, and Divinity, the same Body incarnate of the Blessed Virgin Mary, crucified on the cross, and raised in all of His glory from the dead. Christ's Body in the Eucharist is the same Body that "sits at the right hand of the Father" in heaven. As St. Bonaventure wrote, "There is no difficulty over Christ's being present in the sacrament as in a sign; the great difficulty is in the fact that he is really in the sacrament, as he is in heaven. And so believing this is especially meritorious."[24] The Eucharist is no different than the resurrected Body of Jesus; only the "mode or manner" of Christ's Presence is unique in comparison to how it exhibits in heaven.[25]

Sacred Hosts kept within the same ciborium each contain the Real Presence of Christ. His Body is present within many ciboria, dwelling within the numerous tabernacles, and inside many Catholic Churches throughout the world at this very moment. It is even

[23] Fr. John A. Hardon, *The Real Presence* (Lombard, IL: Inter Mirifica), http://www.therealpresence.org/eucharst/realpres/realpres.htm

[24] In IV Sent., dist. X, P. I, art. un., qu. I.

[25] Fr. James T. O'Connor, *The Hidden Manna: A Theology of the Eucharist,* 2nd Ed. (San Francisco, CA: Ignatius Press, 1988), 285-286.

more profound that He is completely and bodily present even within the smallest particle of each consecrated Host.[26] When a part of the Sacred Host is broken Christ's Presence wholly remains in each part as long as the accidents of bread and wine have not decomposed or have reached a point where they are no longer recognizable[27] under the appearance of bread and wine. Aquinas in his sequence, *Lauda Sion Salvatorem*, for the Mass of Corpus Christi, illustrates this truth in the following stanza:

> When the Sacrament is broken,
> doubt not, but remember,
> that there is just as much hidden in a fragment,
> as there is in the whole.
> There is no division of the substance,
> only a breaking of the species takes place,
> by which neither the state nor stature
> of the substance signified is diminished.

The Church recognizes that Christ is present to the faithful in a multitude of ways, but receiving the Real Presence of Jesus in the Eucharist is a unique and special experience. Pope Paul VI in his encyclical *Mysterium Fidei*, called for the continuous usage of the term transubstantiation, and proclaimed the extraordinary means by which Christ is present in the Eucharistic species:

---

[26] Ibid., 287.
[27] See Aquinas, ST III, q. 77. a. 4.

This presence is called "real" by which it is not intended to exclude all other types of presence as if they could not be 'real' too, but because it is presence in the fullest sense. That is to say, it is a substantial presence by which Christ the God-Man is wholly and entirely present. It would therefore be wrong to explain this presence by taking resource to the "spiritual" nature, as it is called, of the glorified Body of Christ which is present everywhere, or by reducing it to a kind of symbolism as if this most august sacrament consisted of nothing else than an efficacious sign of the spiritual presence of Christ and of his intimate union with the Faithful members of his mystical body.[28]

Catholics are called to believe, and to make a profession of faith in the Real Presence of Jesus in the Eucharist. This dogma is a central tenet to the Catholic faith. The rejection and denial of transubstantiation is a grave sin. Any Catholic who tenaciously refutes or doubts the following decrees, again from the Council of Trent, commits a heresy:

First of all the holy Synod teaches and openly and simply professes that in the nourishing sacrament of the Holy Eucharist after the consecration of the bread and wine our Lord Jesus Christ, true God and man, is truly, really, and sub-stantially (can. I) contained under the species of those sensible

---

[28] Pope Paul VI, Encyclical, *Mysterium Fidei*, 39: AAS 57 (1965). Online at https://www.vatican.va/, CCC 1374.

things. For these things are not mutually contradictory, that our Savior Himself is always seated at the right hand of the Father in heaven according to the natural mode of existing, and yet that in many other places sacramentally He is present to us in His own substance by that manner of existence which, although we can scarcely express it in words, yet we can, however, by our understanding illuminated by faith, conceive to be possible to God, and which we ought most steadfastly to believe. For thus all our forefathers, as many as were in the true Church of Christ, who have discussed this most holy sacrament, have most openly professed that our Redeemer instituted this so wonderful a sacrament at the Last Supper, when after the blessing of the bread and wine He testified in clear and definite words that He gave them His own body and His own blood.[29]

The Catholic Church teaches that:

The Most Holy Eucharist is the most august sacrament, in which Christ the Lord himself is contained, offered and received, and by which the Church constantly lives and grows. The Eucharistic Sacrifice, the memorial of the death and resurrection of the Lord, in which the sacrifice of the cross is perpetuated over the centuries, is the summit and the source of all Christian worship and life; it signifies and effects the

---

[29] Ecumenical Council of Trent, Session XIII, 11 October 1551, Decree on the Most Holy Eucharist, Chapter 1: DS 1636.

unity of the people of God and achieves the building up of the Body of Christ. The other sacraments and all the ecclesiastical works of the apostolate are closely related to the Holy Eucharist and are directed to it.[30]

The Catholic Church defines the Eucharist as the "source and summit of the Christian life."[31] It is the source, because the Eucharist carries out the work of our redemption by making present and offering anew the sacrifice that Christ made on the cross once, and for all mankind.[32] It is the summit, because the Eucharist is the most intimate way that the Blessed Trinity offers us a foretaste of heaven; we receive tomorrow's bread today.

One of the most famous hymns written by St. Thomas Aquinas, "Adore Te Devote," beautifully captivates the theology of the Real Presence of Jesus in the Eucharist. This poetic English translation is by Fr. Gerard Manley Hopkins, S.J.:

Godhead here in hiding, whom I do adore,
Masked by these bare shadows, shape and nothing more,
See, Lord, at Thy service low lies here a heart
Lost, all lost in wonder at the God thou art.
Seeing, touching, tasting are in thee deceived:
How says trusty hearing? that shall be believed;
What God's Son has told me, take for truth I do;

---

[30] Code of Canon Law: Latin-English Edition, Washington, DC: Canon Law Society of America, 1983), 897.

[31] See CCC 1324.

[32] See CCC 1364.

Truth Himself speaks truly or there's nothing true.

On the cross Thy godhead made no sign to men,

Here Thy very manhood steals from human ken:

Both are my confession, both are my belief,

And I pray the prayer of the dying thief.

I am not like Thomas, wounds I cannot see,

But can plainly call thee Lord and God as he;

Let me to a deeper faith daily nearer move,

Daily make me harder hope and dearer love.

O thou our reminder of Christ crucified,

Living Bread, the life of us for whom he died,

Lend this life to me then: feed and feast my mind,

There be thou the sweetness man was meant to find.

Bring the tender tale true of the Pelican;

Bathe me, Jesu Lord, in what Thy bosom ran

Blood whereof a single drop has power to win

All the world forgiveness of its world of sin.

Jesu, whom I look at shrouded here below,

I beseech thee send me what I thirst for so,

Some day to gaze on thee face to face in light

And be blest for ever with Thy glory's sight. Amen.[33]

According to the latest Pew Research Survey the majority of individuals who identify as Catholic do not believe in transubstantia-

---

[33] "Rhythmus ad SS. Sacramentum," in *Poems of Gerard Manley Hopkins*, 3rd ed. (New York, NY: Oxford University Press, 1948), No. 131, 186-187.

tion, the core teaching of the faith. They do not accept the truth of the Real Presence of Jesus in the Eucharist, which imitates the erroneous opinion of Berengarius of Tours in the eleventh century, who held the view that Christ was only present in the Eucharist in a symbolic way.[34] It is a fact that 69 percent of Catholics reject that when they receive Holy Communion they are consuming the Flesh and Blood of Christ, which means that only 31 percent of Catholics believe in the Real Presence. The bread and the wine are believed to be merely a symbol, and do not actually become the True Food and True Drink of Christ.

Out of the number of Catholics who do not believe in the Real Presence of Jesus in the Eucharist, the majority, which is 43 percent, have the understanding that the Eucharist is a symbol and not the actual Body and Blood of Christ, is the position of the Church. When surveying Catholics who are practicing Catholics, and who attend Mass at least once a week the number was about one-third or 37 percent for those who do not believe in the Real Presence in comparison to 63 percent who do accept the Church's teaching.[35]

The belief that the Eucharist is only a symbol directly contradicts the very words of Jesus Himself at the Last Supper when He instituted the Eucharist as a sacrament.

---

[34] "Berengarius of Tours," *Catholic Encyclopedia*, (1907). Online at newadvent.org/cathen/02487a.htm

[35] Gregory A. Smith, "Just one-third of U.S. Catholics agree with their church that Eucharist is body, blood of Christ," Pew Research Survey, (2019). Online at https://pewresearch.org/fact-tank/2019/08/05/transubstantiation-eucharist-u-s-catholics/

> While they were eating, Jesus took bread, said the blessing, broke it, and giving it to his disciples said, "Take and eat; this is my body." Then he took a cup, gave thanks, and gave it to them, saying, "Drink from it, all of you, for this is my blood of the covenant, which will be shed on behalf of many for the forgiveness of sins. (Matthew 26:26-28)

It is before Jesus offers His own Body and Blood, that He gives Himself to us as daily bread, the heavenly food that will nourish us in the wilderness of our lives as we journey towards the eternal Promised Land just as the manna in the desert sustained the Israelites until they reached the promised land of Canaan. This Bread of the Angels does not simply offer us physical nourishment like the manna in the desert, but it provides us with a spiritual nourishment for our minds and souls. This food offers us eternal life and truth as Jesus is, "The way, and the truth, and the life" (John 14:6).[36]

Disbelief of the Real Presence is not a new phenomenon. In John 6, the Bread of Life Discourse, Sacred Scripture brings us to the scene where Jesus is preaching in the synagogue in Capernaum. It is only a short time after the multiplication of the loaves and the fishes when the crowds follow him across the sea coming on boats from Tiberias, near the place where Jesus performed the miracle. As they enthusiastically await and anticipate receiving another source of physical nourishment, they are shocked to hear the words spoken by Him:

---

[36] Fr. Phillip Michael Tangorra, *Holiness and Living the Sacramental Life* (Ohio: Emmaus Road, 2017), 187.

Jesus said to them "Amen, amen, I say to you, unless you eat the flesh of the Son of Man and drink his blood, you do not have life within you. Whoever eats my flesh and drinks my blood has eternal life, and I will raise him on the last day. For my flesh is true food, and my blood is true drink. Whoever eats my flesh and drinks my blood remains in me and I in him." (John 6:53-56)

Christ exhorts His disciples to "eat His Flesh," and "drink His Blood," which reveals the sacrament of sacraments, the Eucharist; because it makes present again the one and same sacrifice that Christ offered once and for all mankind on Calvary, which culminates with Christ in all His glory ascending to the Father in heaven, truly reconciling humanity to Divinity.[37]

When the followers of Jesus respond with "This saying is hard; who can accept it?" (John 6:60),[38] He does not confirm their misunderstanding, but reasserts His Real Presence with this response to them:

"Does this shock you? What if you were to see the Son of Man ascending to where he was before? It is the spirit that gives life, while the flesh is of no avail. The words I have spoken to you are spirit and life." (John 6:61-63)

---

[37] See CCC 1406, 1419.
[38] CCC 1336.

It is only God who can grant eternal life, and by His words Jesus emphasizes that by having a human nature alone He would not be able to offer the gift of eternal life. However, united with His Divine nature, the Eucharist gives eternal life in Him Who is God.

Further confirmation that Christ is referring to His Real Presence in the Eucharist is that when He reemphasizes His previous statement to the Jews concerning the "eating of His Flesh," instead of using the word γεῖν (*phagein*), which is the standard Greek verb used to describe humans eating a meal,[39] and that He had used previously in His discourse, He chooses instead to use the Greek word τρώγω (*trógó*). The term translates to "chew"or gnaw" and is used to describe the means by which herbivores eat.[40] Jesus is utilizing more graphic imagery for the disciples to better understand and to abandon any doubt that He truly means the eating of His Flesh, but in a vegetarian manner. Our Lord knew that what He was teaching them was radical, and that many of His followers would reject His Presence in the Eucharist, and so He wanted to bring clarity to His message.

Many of Jesus' followers could not accept the truth, and from that day forward no longer accompanied Jesus (John 6:66-71). The disciples walking away from Him after He spoke of the Bread of Life reaffirms the Eucharist is not a symbol, but is truly the Flesh and Blood of Christ, because they would not have abandoned Him with

---

[39] "Strong's Greek: 5315 phago," Thayers Greek Lexicon, Electronic Database, (2011). Online at https://biblehub.com/greek/ 5315.htm

[40] "Strong's Greek: 5176 trógó," Thayers Greek Lexicon, Electronic Database, (2011). Online at https://biblehub.com/greek/ 5176.htm

such feelings of disgust if they thought He was speaking figuratively, and not in a literal way.

Another reason we know that Jesus is not speaking metaphorically about his Real Presence in the Eucharist is because at the time Jews commonly used the idiomatic phrases "to eat the flesh" or "drink the blood" to mean "betray, persecute, and murder."[41] There is evidence of such in Sacred Scripture that illustrates how whenever there is a reference to the "eating of flesh" or the "drinking of blood" it is symbolically referring to "betrayal, persecution, and murder" (see Micah 3:3; Psalm 27:2; Isaiah 9:20, 49:26). If Jesus' words to the apostles from John 6 are changed to symbolically read how the Jews would have interpreted them, they would read, "Amen, amen, I say to you, unless you persecute and betray the Son of Man, you do not have life within you. Whoever commits violence against me has eternal life, and I will raise Him on the last day." If Jesus' words were meant to be taken symbolically then what He told His disciples would not have made any sense.[42]

This means "that to receive in faith the gift of his Eucharist is to receive the Lord himself."[43] St. John Damascene affirmed:

The bread and wine are not a foreshadowing of the body and blood of Christ—By no means!—but the actual deified body

[41] Jason Evert, *How to Defend Christ's Presence in the Eucharist*, Catholic Answers (San Diego, CA: Catholic Answers, 2001). Online at https://www.catholic.com/magazine/print-edition/how-to-defend-christs-presence-in-the-eucharist

[42] Ibid.

[43] See CCC 1336.

of the Lord, because the Lord Himself said: 'This is my body';
not 'a foreshadowing of my body' but 'my body,' and not 'a
foreshadowing of my blood' but 'my blood.' [44]

The Church's steadfast belief in the Real Presence of Christ is
illustrated in the various forms of worship that Catholics reserve for
the Blessed Sacrament, which includes Exposition, Adoration, and
Benediction of the Eucharist, Eucharistic Processions, and the Forty
Hours Devotion. The worship of the Blessed Sacrament during
times outside of the Holy Sacrifice of the Mass directly relates to the
Holy and Divine Liturgy, the Eucharistic celebration.

Catholics also affirm their faith in the Real Presence by partaking
in specific practices: properly genuflecting with reverence before the
Tabernacle where the Blessed Sacrament is reserved; making a bow
of the head before receiving Holy Communion; abstaining from
food and drink at least one hour before receiving Holy Communion,[45] not receiving Holy Communion unworthily if one is not in a
state of grace, with mortal sin on his soul, until receiving absolution
during the Sacrament of Confession;[46] and remaining in silence as
an act of reverence for the Blessed Sacrament before and after Mass.

---

[44] *The Orthodox Faith*, IV, [PG 94, 1148-49].

[45] *The Mystery of the Eucharist in the Life of the Church*, No. 23, 15
(2022). Online at https://www.usccb.org/resources/mystery-eucharist-
life-church; CIC 919, §1.

[46] See CCC 2120; CIC, 916. The exception is that it is possible to receive
Communion prior to going to confession in cases where there is a grave
need and no opportunity to confess, and the person returns to a state of
grace by making an act of perfect contrition.

Catholics know that Jesus is truly present in the Eucharist because of the words of Christ recorded in Sacred Scripture, and handed down to the apostles as a part of the Deposit of Faith. God has also provided humanity with physical proof to help practicing Catholics grow in their faith in the Real Presence, and fallen away Catholics and non-Catholics to find their way home to Christ waiting for them in the Eucharist. Through many extraordinary and supernatural events pertaining to the Eucharist, the Real Presence becomes a reality to more and more individuals who witness these signs of God, that demonstrate clear evidence of Eucharistic miracles.

The Catholic Church teaches that public revelation has been fulfilled in Christ, and therefore was completed with the death of St. John the Evangelist, the last apostle.[47] The *Catechism of the Catholic Church* explains that a Eucharistic miracle is a private revelation:

Throughout the ages, there have been so-called 'private' revelations, some of which have been recognized by the authority of the Church. They do not belong, however, to the deposit of faith. It is not their role to improve or complete Christ's definitive revelation, but to help live more fully by it in a certain period of history. Guided by the magisterium of the Church, the *sensus fidelium* [collective sense of the faithful] knows how to discern and welcome in these revelations whatever constitutes an authentic call of Christ or his saints

---

[47] See Pope Paul VI, Dogmatic Constitution of the Church, *Dei Verbum*, 4: AAS 42 (1950).

to the Church. Christian faith cannot accept 'revelations' that claim to surpass or correct the revelation of which Christ is the fulfillment, as is the case in certain non-Christian religions and also in certain recent sects which base themselves on such 'revelations'[48]

Eucharistic miracles help believers and even non-believers to become witnesses to the truth, that the consecrated Host truly contains the Real Presence of Jesus. The Catholic Church has approved a number of Eucharistic miracles; one of the most widely known is the one that took place in a church, in Lanciano, Italy during the eighth century.

There was a Basilian monk who lacked faith in the Eucharist, that it truly is the Flesh and Blood of Christ. During the consecration when he was celebrating Mass and pronounced the "words of institution," the bread and wine before his eyes physically appeared to become the Flesh and Blood of Christ.

Many years later Edoardo Linardi, a physician, professor of anatomy and pathological history and of chemistry and clinical microscopy, and former head of the Laboratory of Pathological Anatomy at the hospital in Arezzo, Italy, was the only doctor to have analyzed the relics from the Eucharistic Miracle in Lanciano. He and his assistant Dr. Ruggero Bertelli, were ultimately chosen and received authorization from the Vatican, Archbishop Pacifico Perantoni of Lanciano, and the provincial minister of the Franciscan Conventuals

---

[48] CCC 67.

of Abruzzo, to conduct a study that would enable the Flesh and Blood to be studied at a scientific level.

The findings of the research were that the Flesh and the Blood were truly from a human being, and there was no question that they were from cardiac muscle since Linardi himself held the endocardium within his hand. The blood type was found to be Type AB, and it was declared by the scientist that it was identical to the blood group of the man of the Shroud of Turin, and had characteristics of a man who was of Middle Eastern origin. The study published in "Quaderni Sclavo di Diagnostica Clinica e di Laboratori" in 1971 was later confirmed in 1976 by the Higher Council of the World Health Organization (WHO), and that the phenomenon could not be explained by science.[49]

There have been many other Eucharistic miracles that have taken place even in more modern times, such as a Host that formed red stains, in Legnica Poland (2013), a red substance found on a Host in Tixtla, Mexico (2006), a Host that developed a human face in Chirattakonam, India (2001), and a Host that had the scent of unleavened bread, and had a red blood stain in Sokolka, Poland (2008). The scientific studies for the Eucharistic miracles in Poland and Mexico confirmed that fragments of the hosts were identical to that of cardiac muscle tissue, and that the tissue had alterations that would be present in a person under significant distress or who is nearing death. Research on the Host from the Eucharistic miracle in Mexico also concluded that the reddish substance was blood, and

---

[49] "Physician Tells of Eucharistic Miracle of Lanciano," Zenit, (2005). Online at https://zenit.org/2005/05/05/physician-tells-of-eucharistic-miracle-of-lanciano/

that it came from the hemoglobin and DNA from a human being. It was found that the blood type was AB, which is the same as the blood type discovered from the Host of Lanciano, Italy, and the Shroud of Turin.[50]

Eucharistic miracles do not contradict the faith of the Church, but confirm Her teaching of the Real Presence of Jesus in the Eucharist. They are supernatural and divine interventions from God that show how we must look beyond the physical appearance of the bread and the wine, and see the substance, the reality, that which is the Flesh and Blood of Christ. These miracles are performed by the Lord to offer a visible sign to humanity, that in the Eucharist we truly find the Body and Blood of Christ.

It is of grave importance that Catholics believe in the Real Presence of Jesus in the Eucharist; that a stupendous miracle takes place at every Catholic Mass, following the command of Jesus, the spoken words of the priest celebrant. Members of the Mystical Body of Christ need to understand that they are receiving God-Incarnate, the Word Made Flesh in the Eucharist. The Real Presence is hidden within a tiny, white, consecrated host, invisible to the five senses. It is by the gifts of faith and grace that the doctrine of the Real Presence can be accepted as truth.

The Real Presence is an act of unsurpassing love that Christ has offered to humanity when He instituted the Eucharist at the Last Supper. Pope Leo XIII wrote in his encyclical, *Mirae Caritas*:

---

[50] "4 Approved Eucharistic Miracles from the 21st Century," Magis Center, (2022). Online at https://blog.magiscenter.com/blog/approved-eucharistic-miracles-21st-century

And this miracle, itself the very greatest of its kind, is accompanied by innumerable other miracles; for here all the laws of nature are suspended; the whole substance of the bread and wine are changed into the Body and the Blood; the species of bread and wine are sustained by the divine power without the support of any underlying substance; the Body of Christ is present in many places at the same time, that is to say, wherever the Sacrament is consecrated.[51]

The Eucharist is not only a fountain of eternal life; it is God Himself. Christ chose to remain present in the Church in a unique and special way. Since Christ would offer His life for us on the Cross, He no longer would physically remain in visible form in the world. Christ promised to never leave us, so humanity was gifted with His sacrament of love: the Eucharist. Pope Francis at the Vatican's Corpus Christi Mass in June 2020 said in his homily: "He gave us Food, for it is not easy to forget something we have actually tasted. He left us Bread in which He is truly present, alive and true, with all the flavour of His love."[52]

The Pope's words reflect upon the Church's teaching of the Real Presence of Jesus in the Eucharist. Christ has given us True Food that the Church will continue to receive by the Lord's command, in

---

[51] Pope Leo XIII, Encyclical *Mirae Caritatis*, 7, (1902). Online at https://www.vatican.va/

[52] See Devin Watkins, "Pope at Corpus Christi Mass: Eucharist Heals our Fragile Memory," Vatican News, (2020). Online at https://vaticannews.va/en/pope/news/2020-06/pope-francis-mass-corpus-christi-eucharist-heals-memory.html

memory of Him, until He comes again in glory, just as what took place on the eve of the Passion.[53] The bread, offered to humanity, becomes Christ Who is Present to us in the Eucharist. We receive His living Body, the whole Christ, as a pledge of his love.[54]

The Real Presence enables Christ to remain with us in our midst in a mysterious way as the one Who infinitely loved us and sacrificed Himself by paying the ultimate price for our sins. He remains with us under signs that illustrate and convey this endless love.[55] St. Peter Julian Eymard reflected upon this Church teaching when he spoke of the Lord sacredly veiled in the Eucharist:

> We can understand why the Son of God loved man enough to become man Himself. The Creator must have been set on repairing the work of His hands. We can also understand how, from an excessive love, the God-man died on the cross. But something we cannot understand, something that terrifies those of little faith and scandalizes unbelievers, is the fact that Jesus Christ after having been glorified and crowned, after having completed His mission here below, wanted still to dwell with us and in a state more lowly and self-abasing than at Bethlehem, than on Calvary itself. With reverence, let us lift the mysterious veil that covers the Holy of Holies and let

---

[53] CCC 1333.
[54] Ibid., 1337.
[55] Ibid., 1380.

us try to understand the excessive love which our Savior has for us.[56]

If only the whole of humanity would strive to return God's love with a fiery zeal that is equal in passion, perhaps more hearts, minds, and souls would be open to accepting the belief in the Real Presence of Christ in the Eucharist.

---

[56] Fr. John A. Hardon, *The Real Presence: Imitation of Christ*, (Lombard, IL: Inter Mirifica). Online at https://realpresencerenewal.org/readings/the-real-presence-imitation-of-christ/.

Chapter 6

The Intellectual Appetite and the Eucharist

Fr. Chris Pietraszko

PART I

MAN DOES NOT LIVE BY BREAD ALONE

Qui respondens dixit: *scriptum est: non in solo pane vivet homo, sed in omni verbo quod procedit de ore Dei.*

Who answered and said: *it is written, not in bread alone does man live, but in every word that proceeds from the mouth of God.*

Matthew 4:4

The world has been lately affected by various dimensions of post-modern philosophy that have an impact on how we approach the Eucharist today. In some ways, the Eucharist, under the philosophy of nominalism, can be reduced to a type of *mere bread*. That is, the nature of the Eucharist becomes nominally related to our lives, because its substance cannot be known, declared, or even experienced. The Eucharist isn't so much known to us as a Mystery of Faith, but rather a type of rationalism that is disconnected from the whole person. Such doubt, and nominal approaches to the sacraments in general, inhibit that reciprocal relationship between faith and the salvific fruits the sacraments[1] intrinsically offer us. It is for this reason that I believe we ought to return to the philosophy and language of the *perennial philosopher*[2] of the Catholic Church: St. Thomas Aquinas. Particularly, we should examine the appetites themselves, because they call to mind the whole person, whereby faith as a virtue assents to this beautiful Mystery. When he speaks about our three appetites, I will apply them to the Eucharist. First, the appetitive nature of man can be investigated by a phenomenological reflection on our experience of Christ in the Eucharist. In this way, man becomes aware of his interior hungers and is able to direct them toward that which ultimately fulfills these appetites. Yet, we need a science to hold our experiences accountable to the truth, and avoid a subjective knowledge disfigured by our wounded, fallen, and fallible nature. Thus, the appetite of the mind involves investigating the causes and effects of the sacraments in such a way that even offers us some language to pierce this mystery. Ultimately the appetites are descriptive of man's nature and avoid a type of nominal discernment of man himself in relation to the Eucharist.

Second, when man can understand his own hunger, he can better understand the Object of his hunger. In this case, when speaking of the intellectual appetite, we discuss principally God being *from whom* this appetite of mankind may find final satiation (or rest).

---

[1] International Theological Commission, *Reciprocity between Faith and Sacraments in the Sacramental Economy*. Online at www.vatican.va

[2] Paul VI, *Optatam Totius* pp 15, 16, 1965. Online at https://www.vatican.va/

Finally, I would like to draw from St. Thomas Aquinas' commentaries of Sacred Scripture in conjunction with his own philosophical anthropology. What seems to be illuminated by a reflection on Aquinas' approach to the Eucharist, and Christ, is one that involves explicit revelatory truths about God, which lead to our love of Him. This type of knowledge, where the human soul consummates with God, allows us to thereby enter into a fruitful relationship in the liturgical act of Eucharistic adoration and worship. In other words, the reciprocity between faith and the sacrament of the Eucharist becomes of pastoral significance. This relationship with Christ, which avoids the vagaries of nominalism, will also help us more deeply understand the Church's mission to evangelize.

Nominalism and Negation

One thing that should be stated at the dawn of this paper pertains to the *limits* of knowledge about God. Knowing the quiddity or essence of God is impossible for the human race in this life, according to St. Thomas. This is simply the case because of God's Divine Simplicity.[3] When using analogical language about God, we still find limits. This leaves us to a certain degree in the dark about *what* and *who* God is. Nonetheless, there is a type of knowledge that we are aching for that pertains to God, and it is in this sense that we speak about a type of satiation of the intellectual appetite. The type of nominalism that I'm supposing here that negatively affects our relationship with Christ and the Eucharist is that which denies God as a

---

[3] St. Thomas Aquinas, *On Essence and Being* at https://isidore.co/

knowable, first cause. Without ascribing to the possibility of cause-effect relationships, we cannot know God as a first principle to all of creation, the meaning of our lives, our relationships, the Mystery of Faith, and of everything good. Aquinas admits that even of natural objects, such as a gnat, we cannot exhaust their essence. Nonetheless there is a general type of knowledge we can have of things, especially in regard to the first principles. It is only in this sense that as humans, our natural intellectual appetite pertains to God. For many, a relational context with God seems to be absent when we discuss causes and effects. This is because these causal relationships have been sterilized from a relational context, and modern man has been habituated in fostering a dichotomy between such Wisdom and Love. In reality, the very basis for a relationship in man often relies upon some notion of a cause or an effect (but perhaps by another name). And its in this sense, that we must reintegrate the intellectual appetite's longing for the ultimate cause of all things into his own spiritual dispositions. When we recognize, for instance, that God has a motive for changing the bread and the wine into Himself, we immerse the whole person in the very generous movement of God's own actions. When we consider that God created the world out of no need for Himself, we arrive at the fact that His act was one of Love. These truths illuminate the mystery of God Himself, and help us to understand the mystery as one of relationship. The scientific examination, which is a speculative virtue, enables us to internalize our own experiences of grace in a rightly ordered manner. In a way that honors the beauty of God's own work.

Furthermore, it is by grace that the intellectual appetite longs to know the quiddity of God. This is a significant improvement upon the human race, and will be assumed to be the manner in which our intellectual appetite is configured. By grace, mankind becomes capable of knowing God's essence, in the life of the blessed. This moves us from seeking to know God as the ultimate cause of all things, to knowing Him in Himself. Thus, by grace we come to a movement within ourselves where we seek to know as much as possibly can about God, and so we come to love everything about Him.

A nominal approach to God, versus the negative and analogical approach Aquinas offers us is worth reflecting on. The nominal approach to God never seeks to pierce the mystery of Him, while the negative and analogical humbly attempts to do just this. What God has revealed, even if it is understood through analogical names, or negative statements, arouses within man a deeper desire to behold the one we love. Thus, what we can know in this negative and analogical sense is the type of knowledge that sets forth a disposition worthy of heaven. Thus, we can say at the same time that we have come to understand the mystery, while it nonetheless stays a mystery. Nominalism on the other hand would set up a type of indifference towards God's essence, and consequently an indifference toward the object of another's faith, and a deadening to the zeal of evangelization. This is typically the case, because there is an automatic suppression of the desire to know God, given that the mind has learned to despair in such a possibility of even natural beings.

The significance of the incarnation enables us to grasp a sacramental type of knowledge, since Christ is the image of the invisible God. Through the revelation of Christ's Paschal Mystery, mankind is able to encounter through the quiddity of His own humanity, the sacrament or visible sign of the very mind of God. Having an encounter with Christ who is the primordial sacrament, we note that Divine-Person is united to a human nature. Witnessing that unity in Christ enables man to *receive* a greater knowledge of God's will, intention, and goodness. We know of God's will that He is seeking a relationship, our salvation, and communion, and He takes up residence in our own world, and in the Eucharist, our body and soul. We become familiar with Him, in such a way that we can identify His voice, and follow Him when He speaks. We learn that God is one who cares to nourish us with Himself, and seeks to address our longings. This incarnate Christ, placed in a manger communicates that He is our bread. In Christ becoming our Bread, we see a very direct link to the appeal, by God, to man's appetite. Christ is concerned about man's hungers, and thus, I use the *appetitive* language as a particular way of appealing to our goodwill that seeks that none may go hungry.

The Three Appetites

Appetite is one of the most basic experiences within the human person—the experience of hunger. Little children, even before they can use words, are capable of communicating their own hunger. Their own body itself is inclined to grow (natural appetite) and seeks to be nourished from the bosom of his or her mother (sensual appetite). Yet, there is still another appetite that exists within each person: an appetite for the *Logos*.[4] When children develop their capacity

---

[4] ST I q80 a1.

to reason, to question, the term *why* incessantly arises. St. Thomas Aquinas would describe this appetite of inquiry to only be satiated in God, who ultimately explains all things, including the person, and all relationships.

It is important to pause for a moment and qualify that the intellectual appetite is not to be reduced to a mere hunger for an extrinsic-dialectic. Such a sterilized notion discourse places wisdom in a book rather than in the mind of the person. In other words, we are avoiding the notion that the intellectual appetite is reduced to rest in mere information that seems to be disconnected from interiorizing, from virtue, and from meaning. An internalist position[5] needs to be assumed here; otherwise we are adopting that very nominalism that only speaks around reality, but is never consummated with its substance. For an extrinsic-dialectic approach to knowledge, there is a tendency to generate a duality between the mind and the heart. In other words, the other type of nominalism we are seeking to avoid is that which is applied to our own essence or anthropology. For man to become rationalistic, and evade the interior dispositions of virtue is to approach our faith without ascribing to a fully human notion of ourselves. Man, with his whole being, must come to know God. But if we do not expose the entirety of man to the truths of our faith, then internally, we have a nominal relationship with God.

---

[5] Cf. Peter A. Pagan, "Natural and Supernatural Modes of Inquiry: Reason and Faith in Thomistic Perspective," *Faith, Scholarship, and Culture in the 21st Century,* eds. Alice Ramos and Marie I. George (Notre Dame: American Maritain Association, 2002), pp. 57-72. Online at https://maritain.nd.edu/ama/Faith/faith103.pdf

People today speak about moving from the "head to the heart," as if these dimensions are somehow autonomously related. Yet for Aquinas, knowledge of the good causes the affect to move toward that good, in love of that good. The dichotomous phenomenon is explained if man is only operating within a nominal type of knowledge, whereby the essence of things is genuinely not internalized. Thus, a person, in a Thomistic sense, could only be aware or capable of meditating on some vague and superficial exterior of things. For Aquinas, however, the intellectual appetite really turns our attention to two main things: knowledge and love,[6] in such a manner that is integrated and internalized. This is important to consider as we reflect on Christ's own temptations regarding the essence of man, and His hungers. The reason becomes clear when we recognize that the temptations Jesus faced were ultimately an attack on His humanity, His identity, and His mission. When nominalism touches these dimensions, the essence of our nature, our worship, our hungers, and our relationships with one another are obscured and vandalized by vagueness and abstractions. This is the type of vagueness that undermines the concrete, revelatory dimensions that actually save us, inform our faith, and enable us to encounter the mystery of God in worship of Christ in the Eucharist.

Temptations Regarding the Intellectual Appetite

The temptations that Jesus faces in the desert all touch on His own natural, passible human appetites. When Jesus refutes the devil,

---

[6] ST I q82 a3.

He calls to mind that while bread satiates an appetite within man, He, as a loving provider, is also concerned with the deepest, most spiritual appetite within man. St. Thomas Aquinas refers to this as the *intellectual appetite*. It is interesting to note that Christ sees this temptation as an attack on the whole of the human race, rather than simply pertaining to his particular experience of hunger. This is evidenced in His response where He uses the term "man." Here, just as in the Garden, God is speaking and making a *universal*, anthropological claim about mankind. He does not say, "I," but rather understands this temptation to ultimately be at the root of His ministry, where the Father, whose Divine Will the Son will accomplish, seeks to *provide for* His hungry children. That is to say that the very mission of Christ is to address our hungers, and here the temptation is for Christ to imagine that our universal ache is reduced to mere bread. The ache must be maintained as more than what our sensory appetite is inclined toward, but rather a relational knowledge and love of God.

Knowledge, to Aquinas, is a spiritual and relational reality. We come to know persons. Something unique is taking place when man comes to know, not only created objects, but subjects or human persons, and most especially Divine Persons.

Considering simple knowledge is worthwhile. Consider children picking up worms, and forgetting about their dirty hands. They stare in wonder and awe at *something* (a transcendental), and that *something* elicits questions that desperately need answers. This transcendental experience of a created thing elicits a deep mystery that desires to be solved: What caused this? How does it work? Why does it exist? This type of knowledge is ultimately moved by a quest for meaning, harboring within the intellect anything but indifference toward the created universe. This child echoes the same expression the Israelites did when they picked up in wonder the bread (not to be confused with "Wonder Bread") that came down from heaven: "What is it?"[7] This mysterious miracle of creation instills in man his investigative inquiry that wants to know. Why? Because what we come to know is good—creation is good. We, as created things, look to creation to know it better, and in that, we come to love it better.

Conflating Creation with the Creator

Yet, as Aquinas suggests, this appetite is never entirely quenched until it arrives at what is *ultimately good*. He says it thus: "God is the last end of man."[8] That is to say, man's intellectual appetite cannot be quenched by mere bread, or by a good that is merely *created*. Aquinas explains that our soul cannot find perfect rest even in the angels, as good as they truly are.[9] There is something about our intellectual appetite that can only rest in the Unmoved Mover, in the cause of all things, in the source of all good. For many, this can be understood coldly, and seems irrelevant to the realm of relationship. The Unmoved Mover, however, elicits further questions pertaining to His will, which is known to be love and an act of grace. From the very act of graciousness, God creates out of *nothing* and *love*. Thus,

---

[7] Ex. 16: 15
[8] ST I-II q 1 a8
[9] *ST* I-II q2 a8.

at the very dawn of our existence we not only arrive at some cosmic explanation of what caused us to physically come-to-be. Rather, integrated into this very question we arrive at the relational dimensions of a God who freely created us for our own sake. Coming to know the will of God in this regard is to begin to love our Creator, rather than some impersonal cause. To speak of God in this way would be to speak *about* or *around* God in a manner that is nominal. However, revelation does not merely offer us reflection on the effects caused by God as if the effect were nothing more than what results subsequent to God. The relationship between cause and effect is an intimate one, where the cause of things contains the very actuality of its effect in other things. In other words, when God creates, redeems, and loves us, something already within Him is extended to us. Whereas within nominalism, cause-effect relationships really amount to before-after, and nothing more. When we understand that God *willed* us *to be*, we understand that what was in Him is now in us, albeit in a finite manner. We share in God's own goodness. Today we hear the terms cause-effect in a very dry, and non-spiritual manner. But we cannot begin to grasp motives, or that everything *depends* upon God. When united to his will, these cannot help but underpin the crucial relational dimensions we have with God. If however, cause-effect relationships are merely a matter of before-after, then there is nothing that intrinsically ties the Uncreated to the Created. Scotus made this error in one of his objections[10] to St. Thomas Aquinas. He forgot that to St. Thomas, the relation-

---

[10] Bl. Duns Scotus, *Duns Scotus Philosophical Writings*, Trans. Allan Wolter, O.F.M. (Hackett Publishing Company: Indianapolis, 1987), 23.

ship wasn't so much between Uncreated (which pertains to God's necessary existence), but rather a relationship of Creator-Created (cause-effect).

An additional disconnect, and more relevant to this chapter, pertains to the Eucharist. Many claim that there is no *substantial* difference between praying at home or in nature and worshiping in a Church. Here, one begins to treat the *effects* of the Divine Good (creation) as though they were the same as consummation with the Divine Good Himself. We are like little children who forget about the love that inspired a gift. We forget the Giver and worship the gift; likewise, creation is a sacrament that is designated to point us toward God! The gift of creation is meant to point us toward the supreme gift of God Himself. Many will object to the obligation to attend Mass since they say, "God is everywhere." Yet this objection is actually a conflation of God's presence by way of power, and His very substantial presence. In this life, however, a deep cultivation of a longing to be united to God Himself is salvific, because it avoids the idolatry of placing created things above Him. The Eucharist, in this sense, if interior worship is rightly established, preserves the interior seeking of God as our last end, in contrast to those things which are effects of God's activity. Here is the temptation: Man does not live *for* bread alone—that is, he does not live *for* the mere effects of God's creating hand. Man's intellectual appetite is inclined to something even greater: the One who created all things, out of nothing and out of love.

It is important to note that those who encounter the Lord through His effects are meant to be drawn directly to God through them. In this sense, we cannot diminish the importance of encountering the Lord outside of the Liturgy. After all, if we fail to see Christ in the poor, in our daily work, in those acts of obedience in our private lives, we do not really bring a pleasing sacrifice to the Lord. Our participating in the liturgy is not only to be valid, and licit, but also fruitful. Fruitfulness is sometimes not a preoccupation, but a mere rigid and de facto approach to the sacraments. The change, conversion, growth, and charity increasing in the soul are called to be something the sacraments effect is us. The sacraments lead to salvation, by interiorly conforming the heart and mind to Christ. Without an integration between the world outside of Mass and Mass, spiritual disorder arises, and fruits are diminished.

When Jesus says, "Not in bread alone does man live, but in every word that proceeds from the mouth of God," (Matthew 4:4) He validates the importance of bread, but also integrates the deeper hunger as well: the hunger He has principally come to address. Jesus, who is the Word made Flesh, ultimately is that Word that comes from the Father's mouth. This is possible when God reveals Himself to us, and our intellectual appetite is satiated by both a knowledge and love of Him. Here is the ultimate point: we cannot love what we do not know. Yet, through faith in God as a Mystery, what we do know of God will naturally elicit a desire to know more, in order to love more! When we know God as our first cause in this relational sense, we seek to know Him more. By grace, we also come to desire to know the very quiddity of God, in the life of the blessed. But in whatever God reveals about Himself, we open the mouth of our intellectual appetite and receive Him with joy. Applying this to the Eucharist is simply done when we consider how many people unaffected by reception of the Eucharist while simultaneously not having faith in the True Presence. It would be like a person hearing a compliment, but distrusting it simultaneously. The compliment cannot be received in a spiritual sense, since the faith in its substance is not present. This reveals to us the very damning event that takes place every time we simply try to get the sacraments of initiation "done." The Church becomes a dispenser of a Sacrament received as grace in vain (at least at that moment). This is nothing worth celebrating, and can in fact be a sacrilege.

Let us now return to the temptation. At the very dawn of temptation in the desert, the devil seeks to assert an anthropology that reduces us to mere beasts. And if not beasts, merely contented with created things, such as bread. Our intellectual appetite is merely sidestepped, as though our only appetite is natural and sensual. Satan wants to see the human race starve spiritually, and is content if we do this while our bellies our full.[11] The temptation here deals with Jesus' ministry—to tempt Jesus to ultimately address the temporal needs of our animal nature (and later to only address the political ones). But the devil does not want us to explicitly hunger for Christ, or at best, seeks to obfuscate our self-understanding of that hunger. This has ramifications for the Church, who shares in the mission of Christ Himself. If our hungers are not explicitly known to us, we find ourselves lost, and wayward! Furthermore, evangelization becomes entirely irrelevant, because that universal ache and appetite for Christ is unknown even to the evangelizers. If we do not know the hunger in ourselves for God we cannot rightly empathize for the

---

[11] John 6:12.

scattered sheep who go hungry for Him. Our evangelization becomes normatively an anonymous or nominal effort, and our practice has more to do with culture or nominal effects on our lives. Concretely, we talk around the name of Jesus—very much unlike what we see on display in the Acts of the Apostles. Perhaps we end up living even in an ecclesial culture that is more likely to take His name in vain than to speak it with the affection and reverence the Holy Name itself signifies. Much of this is the fruit of simply living in the mode of a dead version of Christendom.

The Flesh

When we become unaware of what we are hungering for, it is natural to use our experience and consider what has filled us prior. Sensual pleasures can often be where our mind moves first when remembering satiation. And for this reason, when there is an ache within the intellectual appetite in conjunction with an ignorance of that ache, it happens often that we turn to the *flesh*. We are essentially *looking for love in all the wrong places.* Satan knows that by obstructing our knowledge, our awareness of this deepest hunger, we will turn in unbearable hunger to the addictive reality of the flesh. When the flesh, which the Master tells us is of no avail, is appeased, we are numbed and rendered unaware of that suppressed, deeper longing. We in effect suppress what makes us different than the beasts, and morally lose touch with our dignity.

Consider our world today: the growing reality of atheism, and the various gods that inadequately address our intellectual appetite.

Consider Netflix as a business experiencing incredible success at the onset of the pandemic. Consider the slogans we find in our movie theatres that offer us "escape." All of this is because man has somehow been fooled into thinking that he seeks mere bread alone. That is to say, the object of the will is disordered when it is deeply seated in created things. We are looking for rest in the flesh, but to no avail.

Aquinas' Three Pieces of Advice

St. Thomas Aquinas speaks about this temptation, and in his typical manner outlines three things to consider from Christ's response. (1) We are to return to scripture; (2) do nothing according to the judgment of the devil; and (3) "that one should not perform useless work just to show his own strength, because this is vanity."[12]

First, Sacred Scripture directly and infallibly addresses the intellectual appetite, because it contains words that come from the Father's mouth. In Sacred Scripture we find clear direction, not only about moral matters, but also and most importantly about the goodness of our God. Not only do we find direction in the praying of scripture, but also an encounter with the voice of God. In this way, the soul is directed toward a type of rest of the appetite, which reposes in God's goodness as revealed.

Second, avoid following the instruction of the devil. While this may seem obvious, it is practically more difficult to live out, when we cannot decipher his voice from Christ's. Keep in mind that is the very nefarious genius of the devil, to present himself as an angel of

---

[12] St. Thomas Aquinas, *Commentary on Matthew*, 103-104 #319.

light. If the nature of God's communication is nominally under-stood, it becomes easy to label something that is good as evil, and something that is evil as good. We arrive at the phenomenon which St. Ignatius speaks of, in the learning to discern our own voice, the voice of the devil, the world's voice, and finally God's infallible voice. Yet, with nominalism, the essence of these voices cannot be known. God is some unknowable mystery, which seems to unlock for us the ability to interpret His will as we please, entirely disconnected from divine and natural Law. However, when the scientific virtue to dis-tinguish His voice is established in our lives, it is with ease that we hear and follow the Good Shepherd.

Third, St. Thomas seems to think that this temptation attempted to elicit in Christ a need to prove Himself. It is a common, fallen, human experience to doubt our own identity. In this regard the devil begins with the *hypothetical* term "if" and adds, "you are the Son of God."[13] Injecting a hypothetical term into the most important di-mension of Christ's identity—His relationship with the Father—is worth reflecting on. Sometimes, when we are vain, it's because we are actually trying to prove something to ourselves. Our identity is in a perpetual state of the hypothetical,[14] never solidly or concretely anything specific. This can lead to insecurities, and we seek to re-solve this problem by some existential over-compensating. This over-compensation or fearful response ends up best being described as seeking vain-glory. This hypothetical relationship with ourselves,

---

[13] John 4:3.

[14] Robert Spaemann and Holger Zaborowski, *"An Animal That Can Promise and Forgive."* Online at https://www.communio-icr.com/

God, and reality is therefore incredibly harmful. In effect, because man is now hypothetical in relationship, not only to others but also to himself, he easily becomes a chameleon to each given circumstances, and this change is guided by the winds of passion. When we do this, we can free ourselves to act according to the movement of our passions rather than our ontological configuration toward what is true and good. This ultimately suppresses the specific difference within our humanity: the intellectual appetite. Jesus explains that those who have failed to accept His teaching on the Eucharist were operating in the hermeneutics of the flesh,[15] and thus many have found his teaching difficult.[16]

Thankfully Christ knew exactly who He was—and did not need to prove Himself to anyone. He understood that the Father would glorify Him. This confidence within Christ is also a type of rest, but it is rooted in the Father, in the supernatural end, resting in His Father. Since Christ's mission is the Church's it becomes evident that the Church herself will undergo a temptation to question her own identity. The Church might forget her identity as not merely being some organism or community, but also Christ's Body.[17] In this regard, the Church must be confident against any hypothetical terms applied to her identity and the Eucharist, which cannot be defined apart from His Body.

In these three ways, St. Thomas Aquinas seems to be addressing the supernatural appetite within the human race. Christ does not

---

[15] John 6:63.

[16] John 6:60.

[17] Pope Benedict XVI, *The Church: Christ's Body, not Ours.* Online at www.ewtn.com

respond by speaking about Himself. He does not say, "*I do not live by bread alone.*" Rather Christ makes an anthropological (universal) claim and answers on behalf of everyone. In this way, His temptation is our own, and His rebuke is also our own to internalize. We rest in considering the voice of God alone, which is manifest in scripture, and a relationship with the Father. What is fascinating and perhaps worthy of consideration is that when Christ is tempted, He does not experience this merely as an individual. Rather there is a direct connection to the whole of the human race! We see here, therefore, that there is a character of a moral act that always elicits "man" rather than just "I." Simply put, man is morally always social, and connected to his brothers and sisters when tempted.

Consequently, both the world and Christ have a shared mission in addressing the appetites of "man." Christ's method is not through the vain consumeristic toil of labor (as though we get our identity and value from being a cog in the machine). Rather, as we approach a day of rest, we find ourselves flourishing as human beings, with our appetites more rightly ordered to that end which we are called. In this way, Christ seeks not to suppress our appetites, but to unbind them from the foolery of seeking mere bread and vain-glory. It is nonetheless that the liturgy itself can become exactly those things which He asks us to be unbound from. Mass can become a performance and matter of mere optics that draws attention away from God to some matter of the flesh. We ought to ask, therefore, when coming to mass: Who are you looking for?

PART II

WHO ARE YOU LOOKING FOR?

"…Men often want as their ruler someone who will provide them with temporal things. Thus, because our Lord had fed them, they were willing to make him their king: *you have a mantle, to be our ruler* (Isa 3:6). Chrysostom says: *see the power of gluttony. They are no longer concerned about his breaking the Sabbath; they are no longer zealous for God. All these things are set in the background now that their bellies are full. Now he is regarded as a prophet among them, and they want to set him on the royal throne as their king.*"[18]

Nominally Approaching Christ

If we do not know Christ, we cannot begin to know the Eucharist since they are one and the same Divine Person. Thus, when Christ speaks about our hungers, which are for Him, He should be generating within us a healthy curiosity about Himself and our own ache. Christ has used bread, which relates analogically to the human intellectual appetite, hungering for Him. Yet there are other intellectual hungers occurring within human life, including our nature to be political, social, and moral creatures. These human creations— civilization, politics, leadership, and voluntary behavior—are nonetheless analogical to *mere bread*. That is to say, they are not God— and therefore they cannot be where our appetite is finally satiated.

---

[18] St. Thomas Aquinas, *Commentary on John*, Lecture 6, #870.

In other words, where God uses bread to point toward something higher, we sinfully use it to point to something comparatively baser.

Consider that the people attempt to make Christ a king: this causes Christ to revisit the desert, where He is tempted to worship Satan in order to inherit the kingdoms of the world. It is beneath Christ's dignity to receive a kingdom from anyone but His Father. We therefore find ourselves at another place of confusion and disorder in the intellectual appetite. Consider a cultural habituation, or dare I say *obsession* with politics. None of this is to say that politics or policies are unimportant, but any structure we build apart from grace is insufficient for salvation. Christ shuns this, because again they denigrate *the Bread that came down from Heaven*, to something of human invention.

In some ways, the people did not get to know Jesus; they simply saw the before and after-math of His works. This example of a nominal relationship with Christ—where we are not preoccupied with *who* and *what* He is—is centered rather on what He can do for us. This shortsighted approach is also irreverent because it disposes us to *use* God for our own ends. Our worship of Him becomes entirely contingent upon our understanding of His every decision and approval thereof. Interpreting Christ through the flesh of politics becomes the hermeneutics which twist and turn around the very meaning of Christ's own teaching. From this we get doctrines such as *liberation theology*, despotic rulers, and utopian visionaries.

A Veiled Hunger for Christ, and His Hunger for Our Faith

Christ was placed into a manger because He is food for the whole world. He is ultimately *who* our intellectual appetite hungers for anthropologically and by grace. In this sense we cannot understand the intellectual appetite of mankind to find its satiation in a non-internalistic dialectic, but rather a personal *Logos*, consummated with our nature. It is a type of *relational knowing* and *loving* that brings genuine satiation to the intellectual appetite. This can be understood when we consider that another term for the intellectual appetite is simply "the will." Without a will, we cannot be considered persons, and therefore cannot understand personal relationship. This deliberate and appetitive dimension in man is ontologically integrated, and not dichotomous. That is, man does not choose apart from relationships because when he acts, he acts as a person. In this sense, we have a personal relationship with Truth. This helps us understand why the Logos is Himself personal. When one experiences the transcendental dimension of truth, it is not merely some type of nominal knowledge occurring. Rather, such truth is consummated in the intellect, and is then treasured in our hearts, as demonstrated by the Virgin Mary.

It is in response to this ontological impulse in mankind—a hunger for a relationship with Christ—that Jesus feeds the five thousand. This very act communicates His desire to be united to us intimately. We must consider how we miss the point here. Every time we consciously or unconsciously reduce the gospel to socialism, secular humanism, or the elation of some policy or political victory, we as a Church are driven back into the desert to be tempted by the same demon who tempted Christ. In reality, it would seem as though this only happens because our own hunger and disposition is veiled from our own conscious awareness. In this case, we are reading scripture from the hermeneutics of a secular hermeneutic of value-system. Analogically, we stand before a refrigerator and uselessly speculate about what we it is we desire, trying all sorts of things, yet never finding satiation (to no avail). Christ is tempted in the desert to become a King, by submitting his worship to Satan who is the prince and ruler of a fallen world. Christ's human will therefore is tempted to divest itself from union with man's last end in God.

A Ministerial, Vicarious Appetite

God has His own type of thirst and hunger in this regard—it is what I would call a *vicarious hunger* for a relationship with us—as though He peers into our soul, recognizing *our* spiritual poverty, and in a supernatural type of empathy and goodwill, makes our hunger His own. He thirsts for the faith of the woman at the well, not because He lacks any perfection or even happiness without our faith, but because He is so close to our longings that He allows them to become His. This is what I mean by a type of vicarious hunger: the Son of God, who is Happiness, only hungers for happiness in a vicarious sense. Consider when you look toward a person without health, and even though you have your own health in good order, you enter into their suffering. Their longings for relief, refreshment, and healing become a sentiment abiding in your own heart and mind. In this sense, God hungers in regard to our intellectual appetite. Simply put, He is not indifferent to His spiritually starving children.

Even while we are often unaware of the object of that incredible ache and restlessness, Christ is entirely aware of it. He allows our aches and pains to affect Him in some mysterious manner. He sees the addictions, distractions and malice of sin as all wayward, yet all rooted in an ontological impulse toward Himself. He is close to those who are so very far from Him, and it's this paradox that might cause us to spiritually swoon. God is perusing us like a groom, His bride. And He is not seeking His own satiation, but ours. He is a true lover of the Church, and seeks our good entirely for our own sake.

For the Church, we are to enter into this type of *ministerial vicarious hunger* for the non-believer and quasi-catechumen.[19] We recognize the universal reality of the intellectual appetite and its Object, but also having experienced intrinsically that ache, likewise empathize for those who hunger in a veiled manner. If we have this vicarious appetite for the faith of others, we gain insight (knowledge) into God's own goodness. If we do not, our relationship with Him becomes nominal. That is to say, those who do not commit themselves to *evangelization* have a type of nominal relationship with God's own interior ache for the faith of others. For this reason, evangelization is a way of better knowing God, and cannot be disjunctive to the call to holiness. For this reason, any radical pluralism naturally places us at odds with a rightly ordered, healthy relationship with the interior life of Christ.

---

[19] St. John Paul II, *Catechesi Tradendae,* pp 44. Online at https://www.vatican.va/

A Mere Prophet

What is our reaction to this impulse of intimate union with the Logos in scripture? We try to make Him a worldly king to solve our political agendas. How lost are we to miss the mark so evident here? It's heartbreaking. St. Thomas Aquinas explains: "…they did not yet have perfect faith, for they believed that Jesus was only a prophet, while he was also the Lord of the prophets. Yet, they were not entirely wrong, because Our Lord called himself a prophet"[20] What is on display here is a concrete example of the effect of incomplete faith. This causes us to examine what St. John Paul II spoke about which remains relevant today: the phenomenon of the quasi-catechumen. The incomplete faith formation of those who have simply "done" some of the sacraments, find themselves with an incomplete understanding of Christ.

Even with the understanding of Christ's superiority, they would still not be able to internalize the miracle He performed, because the cause of that miracle is still a Person veiled. Think of it like this: a child whose parents feed, clothe, and bathe them does not necessarily understand the service, patience, and love they are receiving. It is possible, without a deeper appreciation for their parents, that they might internalize these acts not resulting from the reality of dependency and love. Rather, a child might internalize these acts without gratitude, but entitlement, as though they are to understand their identity as the object of another's service. When the child is raised, it's important to therefore share responsibilities around the

---

[20] St. Thomas Aquinas, *Commentary on John*, Lecture 6, #867.

house with them, otherwise the child will always see themselves as the object of being served rather than serving.

Likewise, when looking to Christ as a mere prophet, we fail to have the righteous degree of appreciation, reverence, and awe in what He is doing in providing us with food. The Supreme Godhead is trying to build a friendship and relationship with us, while also saving us from an unquenched intellectual appetite! This is *good news*; but do we see it that way? It was only when I considered the internal movements of my own parents that I began to appreciate everything they had done for me. I was able to see that I was not the entitled objective of service, but the recipient of generosity, sacrifice, and love. If this is the case in our human relationships, it must be the case with the Divine Persons in an elevated sense. Despite God's perfect, self-sufficiency, and capacity for existing autonomously from the created universe, He willed that I be for my own sake. Then He willed that I be fed by His own hand. Not only am I fed by His own hand, but I am fed the most glorious Bread of Angels. This is something we cannot appreciate when in a relationship with a mere mouthpiece (prophet) of God. A mere prophet is never the ultimate cause of the good news – whereas Christ who is God has become the prophet and the origin of that Good News.

Christ Takes Flight: When the Eucharist No Longer Bears Fruit

What were the effects, if any, of reducing the Son of God to a mere prophet? They try to make Him a political solution to their temporal problems. He becomes a *politicized* personality to cheer their own cause. God thus is subordinated to man's kingdom, and man's will. The "Our Father" prayer is ultimately inverted to say: "Our will be done." This very prayer, occurring in the liturgy when Christ has become present to us substantially, illustrates for us a type of context appropriate to such worship. Yet, when we spiritually invert this prayer, and extrinsically recite this prayer, a type of incompatibility to fruitfully receive Our Lord occurs. Aquinas explains that the effect of their spiritual approach to Him involves, "Christ's flight from them."[21] Take a brief moment to monitor your own heart at the thought of Christ fleeing your presence. Doesn't that strike your heart with a great sadness? We would do well not to internalize this in a manner contrary to His love for us. However, in this act of fleeing, the object of Christ's flight is not so much a union with ourselves, but the mode or type of unity the Jews were seeking with Him.

Unity or communion here has several variations. Some good, some nominal/apparent. Therefore we cannot use the term "unity" as though it were an infallible sentiment that is always and everywhere good, since we live in a type of nominalism, where terms are used without exact meaning. We must understand that the unity God is seeking is one rooted in the reality and depth of His goodness and love. Seeking to build a relationship that diminishes this, is a cause for His flight.

Consider those relationships in your life where people offer empty flattery to serve their own purposes. Or offer you money to control your decisions. What of the gift of power (kingship) to push their agenda? Or a mutual seeking of pleasure without the good? These things have been known to corrupt the Church from within.

---

[21] Ibid., #868.

Being overly concerned with its *public relations* has led to disastrous decisions that have enabled abuse, avoided transparency, and festered unhealed wounds. Even being concerned with PR in the midst of scandal does not call for interior and actual change, but the extrinsic show thereof. All have a right to a *good-name*, because a good-name is a term associated with the objective moral character of the person or community. Yet, where that person or community has an objectively corrupted moral character and it is right to make this known publicly, we enter as a Church into a deceiving political enterprise that merely sweeps issues under the proverbial carpet. A good-name may be helpful in building trust as a foundation to evangelizing, yet such trust must not be nominal or an extrinsic show— but a witness that pierces both words and deeds. In this regard, words and deeds are both extrinsic dimensions, but a witness is where the internal life of the actor is aligned to the spirit of such acts. Thus emphasizing deeds or words over each other ends up being a somewhat dim competition of externals, negating the interior life that supports both when done rightly.

A virtuous person sees these types of relationship, these false-friendships, for what they are: something worth avoiding. This doesn't mean we write off the people who are seeking these things, but it does mean we communicate boundaries, and establish our intentions in the realm of accountability. Is this not the same around all the laws about worthy reception of the Eucharist? Is it not the case that the term "worthy" has nothing to do with earning this gift, but ensuring we receive Christ in a manner that is owed to Christ out of justice? After all, the Eucharist is not an artifact of faith, but a Person. Christ establishes boundaries so that our relationship will not be reduced to something worldly, and therefore fail to address the genuine hungers of the human soul. Christ has boundaries, and we see this in His act of taking flight. Of course, this does not occur as though the Eucharist would grow legs and run from the tabernacle. However, in one manner, the Eucharist will cease to bear fruit for communities and individuals if that same community enters into a spirit of presumption as did the sons of Eli. Christ takes flight in a manner where he ceases to produce fruits. That is to say, we have an local proximity to the Eucharist, but not a spiritual one.

When speaking about worthy reception of the Eucharist, Aquinas writes:

...there are two ways of receiving this sacrament, namely, spiritually and sacramentally. Therefore, some receive sacramentally and spiritually, namely those who receive this sacrament in such a way that they also share in the reality of the sacrament, namely, charity through which ecclesial unity exists. To such the Lord's words apply: *he who eats me will live because of me.* But some receive only sacramentally, namely those who receive this sacrament in such a way that they do not have the reality of the sacrament, i.e., charity. To these are applied the words spoke here: **he who eats and drinks unworthily eats and drinks judgment to himself.**[22]

---

[22] St. Thomas Aquinas, *Commentary on the Letters of Saint Paul to the Corinthians*, C. 11, Lecture 7, #698.

It would therefore be implied here that such *charity*, which cannot in this life exist without *faith* is the assimilating character that enables man to receive the sacrament spiritually and sacramentally. Therefore, without both of these dimensions held together, man would drink condemnation upon himself. Alternatively, when these are together, man learns to gnaw on God in faith and charity. Furthermore, that act of gnawing doesn't occur privately, disconnected from the Body of the Church. Rather, it occurs in the context of unity with God and His community. In this regard, we cannot really understand the Eucharist as an act of worship without drawing upon the whole of the Church, and our social nature outside of the liturgy. When the *unity* within the Church is false or merely apparent, there will not be a fruitfulness to that reception of the sacrament simply because Christ flees *spiritually*. Christ signifies the lack of fruitfulness in such a vain relationship by departing.

Application

We must ponder, wherever the Church fails to produce fruits, why this might be occurring. In a type of examination of conscience we must consider the biblical reasons why this took place and apply them to our own contemporary circumstances with an honest examination. St. Thomas Aquinas establishes for us three reasons why Christ fled: (1) a detraction from His dignity to accept a kingdom from men, (2) it would have caused harm to His teaching, (3) and to teach us to despise the dignities of the world.[23] All are worthy of

---

[23] Aquinas, Lecture 6, #871.

some meditation, because they once again set boundaries over our relationship with Christ, and therefore the Eucharist. When the liturgy forgets its vertical movement, and reduces it to some social tapping of the feet, there is a detraction from the very real dignity or object of the liturgy: Christ. If the liturgy receives its identity from men, rather than Divine Tradition and Sacred Scripture, then it is denigrated to a mere bread, and Christ a mere guru or mere prophet of knowledge. On the other hand, the liturgy is for the sake of mankind—but in accord with giving glory to God, and offering satiation of the spiritual appetites. When the Church reduces her worship to something proposed and initiated by man rather than God, the Church echoes the errors of the people, causing Him to take flight. Keep in mind that Christ is attempting to, by setting these boundaries, rightly order our appetites. He is walking away from us in order to foster a seeking of the actual Jesus we desire.

Consider Eli losing the Ark as it was abused in a fight against the Philistines.[24] Their presumption and moral corruption, which was challenged and went unaddressed, resulted in the Ark of the Covenant being lost. Consider Christ, who under the care of St. Joseph had to flee into Egypt because of Herod's addiction to power. Consider all of the exiles, where God's chosen people were planted on alien soil because of their unfaithfulness. Christ flees us, to call us back to a genuine relationship with Him, and the Eucharist likewise will only bear fruit if we unite ourselves to Him as individuals and a community in the right spirit. There is a type of indictment on our faith where we fail to produce fruits of the Spirit, and this is meant

---

[24] 1 Sam. 4.

to awaken the Church to a genuine examination of conscience. We cannot look to the silver lining (especially if that lining is of worldly sentiments), but we must in all humility expect the problem is on our end, not on the end of a generous God who would never deny anyone the Holy Spirit[25] who asks rightly.[26]

We cannot consider a lack of fruitfulness to simply pertain to the singular act of liturgical worship either. Although abuses may exist, as well as human innovations, any reception of the Eucharist that occurs in mortal sin will not bear fruit. God will not bless a path that leads away from Him. He will harken the harlot back to Him (Ezekiel 16), by driving her into the desert where she must address the root of the problem. Concretely, our private lives therefore become incredibly important to monitor. All of this seems to be taken up in man's appetite towards union with God. We must rightly order our lives in such a way that everything we do, say, and choose is ultimately configured toward union with the very Substance of Christ.

PART III

KNOWING GOD'S WAYS TO AVOID RIGIDITY AND PLURALISM

To despise anything always occurs as a consequence of what we have come to love. If we love the world, we will hate Christ. If we love Christ, we will hate the world. If we love Christ's gospel, we will hate the world's gospel. Although if Christ's way is nominally under-

---

[25] Luke 11:14.

[26] James 4:3.

stood, we can *implicitly* conflate Him with the world. What do I mean by that last statement? Consider how often we use the term "gospel." Sometimes the term seems to be more of a sentiment for secular humanism or some vague shout of optimism. But a clear reference to the content of the *Kerygma* (basic teaching of the Gospel) can often be absent. Likewise, who Jesus is may not be signified by the acclamation of His name. I have encountered well-meaning Catholics who were well into their grandparent years who nonetheless were surprised to discover that Jesus is God! In conversation with them, they laughed at the idea, though they sat in the pews weekly. Once I encountered a man during Mass who, once he had run out of the precious blood, refilled his chalice with unconsecrated wine. When confronted, his response was "it tastes the same." What we are finding is an incomplete faith or a nominal one.

Aquinas' third point therefore comes last because he hopes to first establish in us a love for Christ's identity. If we can identify Christ in the Eucharist, we love Him in the Eucharist! Our worship becomes authentic. When we have love for Him, a despising of worldly power will subsequently occur, because we will internalize it as that mere bread, which offers us emptiness in the intellectual appetite.

It's always worth nuancing that power, honor, pleasure, and wealth are of themselves not evil. But in a very *practical sense*, we must learn to despise them *as* ends in themselves. We should see how these things are either side-effects or a means, and this is well and good. But we must despise them as idols—as ends. Therefore, in practical acts, we must disincline ourselves toward them in order to build a practical preference towards the things of God. Christ, practically, flees power, which gives us an example of spiritual sobriety.

Unveiling the Object of Our Appetite

We are hungering for God, not a mere prophet, and not mere bread. We are hungering for a divine King, and a divine Prophet, and a divine, eternal Priest. To get any of these three wrong is to orient our hunger in the wrong direction, in an end that is apart from man's fulfillment and therefore salvation. It will also distort what and who we receive in the Eucharist, and confuse the Church's mission with the world's.

Man comes to desire what he knows to be good. It is for this reason that we must have an *encounter* with God (the Supreme Good), whereby in our intellect we experience the penetrating substance of the Logos. Breaking into our ship, breaking into our soul, breaking into our lives, we come to know Him, and are invited to follow (love) Him. God accomplished this for me when I attended a youth conference in Steubenville during a period of Adoration. To be brief, God brought about a vivid memory from my past, a place where an unhealed wound existed. There He inserted Himself into the memory and made a place of rejection and hurt a new place of friendship and of Divine Love. When I opened my eyes, there stood before me the priest holding the Monstrance. Awakened within me was a much deeper faith in His true presence, but more than that, the experience of His gaze and the reality of His personal love for me. This particular encounter was later transformed into a habit in my worship as a priest. When I celebrate the Mass, I am deeply (intrinsically) aware of who it is I am genuflecting toward after consecration. My head leans against the altar briefly in order to take a moment and rest in what has just taken place, what Reality is before me. There has yet to be any auto-pilot act of worship in that moment of consecration, and it is rooted all in that past encounter with Him, which remains incredibly new and relevant in my life. His grace doesn't grow old, because it is a living-faith.

Such encounters, facilitated by the members of the Church, and caused by God, occur in various ways. Often these encounters occur outside of the liturgy. Yet, once someone comes to know Christ through faith, they know the Eucharist. Here we see how faith is vital for fruitful participation in the Eucharist. And when we understand that His presence is in the Eucharist, the integrative connection before whom we worship occurs. The encounter is an integrative key to worship that avoids nominal approaches. In this we find someone coming to know Christ, and from that non-nominal knowledge, comes to worship in both *spirit and truth.*[27]

Contemporary Roadblocks: Rigidity and Pluralism

When putting such concrete experiences of grace next to the realities of rigidity and pluralism, it becomes difficult to share our faith. We get trapped in a type of extrinsic ideological narrative or a telescopic spirituality. We have often used the term telescopic philanthropy to describe those who love a vague concept of humanity, but cannot get along with their very real and concrete next door

---

[27] John 4:24.

neighbor. But there is also a type of vague faith that seems to arise that is entirely rationalistic. It fails to involve an encounter with anything but the terms that we use, rather than the very depth of what they indicate. In all such cases we tend to discuss our appetites without quenching them. Had He partially quenched our appetite in the Eucharist, it would produce fruits in our lives that lead us away from such errors. A rigidity that seeks a tradition for its own sake, or a pluralism which worships human unity apart from union with God, all demonstrate a lack of a *substantial* knowledge of the faith.

The novelty of pluralism in our day presents a unique problem to the satiation of our hunger. If any object (i.e. relativism) satiates our hunger, there doesn't seem to be anything universal about man's intellectual appetite. This very view infiltrates the Church when we become indifferent about evangelization. There is an observable and latent desire from within the Church to evangelize. Pope St. Paul VI was able to identify this and to point out that we cannot really be saved as Catholics if we do not evangelize.[28] Here we recognize that part of the appetite is not merely satiated by reception of some mere content, but must by way of a relationship. When we love God, that love diffuses of itself and spreads or overflows. If we have understood evangelization as a mere matter of indoctrinating and catechizing others, we have developed an extrinsic-dialectic approach. The Eucharist, however, is consumed, and Christ is meant to be assimilated (internalized) into our very lives. This act of worship gives us a type of signification of the internalizing process of Christ in our

---

[28] Pope Paul VI, *Evangelii Nuntiandi*, pp 80. Online at https://www.vatican.va/

lives. It demonstrates something contrary to an extrinsic type of indoctrination.

This might cause some to scratch their head, but I suspect that occurs due to the election of an extrinsic-dialectic approach to the faith. I grew up amongst the idea that if we merely explain our teaching, this would be sufficient as a type of evangelization. As though if we were to put the Apostles' Creed onto some sort of billboard, we would be offering people content that ought to naturally cause their conversion. I believe telescopic philanthropy illustrates the same problem—many people are "outraged" about both apparent and real injustices. Yet in this passionate, entirely speculative, and hypothetical approach to the human race, we end up with a method of overcoming those injustices that involve performing more injustices of a different kind. The failure to love what is concrete, and yet remain in nominal vagueness of faith in Christ and the Church's mission, disconnects us from authentic Christian relationships, and reality itself.

Consider the type of ignorance that can govern a person's judgments when they do not serve the poor. A failure to recognize the deep complexity that may exist amongst the homeless and poor. Many have deep mental health issues, sometimes caused by abuse or trauma, and these things can be mixed in with drug abuse. But others flippantly say, "Get a job." There is no knowledge shown in such *ignorant statements*. Why is there such ignorance? If we know that ache existed in God, and we loved God, would not that ache then exist vicariously for others? Would we not share the ache of the one we love most? Our knowledge of God here must then be seen as transmitted in an interpenetration of real relationships between God, ourselves, and others. That is to say, we are having a relationship not with an idea, but with the Logos, with a Person.

Likewise, we cannot know God without knowing His love for others. And we cannot know His love for others, if we do not practically enter into that love for those whom He loves. We cannot know this dimension of God, therefore, if we are unaware of the poor. We cannot know the heart and mind of God in an intrinsic manner, if we do not understand the human condition outside of our own personal lives. There is a type of knowledge therefore that occurs in the concrete action of the celebration of the sacraments, when such acts occur in the context of faith and community.

This example serves as a type of analogy for the very real way man comes to know God as our first cause. God, as our first cause, comes to create, redeem, sanctify, feed, and love us. The pluralist and rigid legalist both seem to adhere to either a latent hatred for the concrete or love abstract rationalism. Neither of these approaches acknowledge[29] the substance of reality or of God. For those who adhere to a hatred (or indifference) of the concrete, they prefer to live in *the world of forms disconnected from reality*. For those who excessively love what is extrinsic, they adhere to these dimensions not because of their actual meaning but the superficial effects. Christ describes the rigid as whitewashed tombs, and the pluralist as lawless. In both cases, an interiorizing of God's ways remain veiled. Our knowledge of God grows by an encounter with Him and then following Him. Both in encountering Him and following him do we

---

[29] Mark 6:20.

learn to internalize God in a manner that ceases to be merely nominal.

St. Thomas Aquinas is not considered a rationalist. He does not approach knowledge as though it were something we could obtain without hinging it upon experiences and encounters. He does not speak of virtue as though it were the mere habituation of externally good acts or external routines. The will, the affect, and the body are all healed and liberated by virtue—it penetrates every aspect of the person. The work of evangelizing, likewise, goes so much deeper than addressing the complexity of the poor—it goes to addressing the complexity of spiritual poverty. This is why there is a danger in those who reduce the gospel to secular humanism or secular social-justice. We fail to actually live out what is *truly right and just*. Likewise, when we omit the community and enter into a private state of worship during the liturgy, we likewise deny our own social humanity, and conformity with the Trinitarian Image, and the concerns of Jesus.

We often live in a culture where we are more likely to take Jesus' name in vain than to use it with the affection and reverence that are due to His name. Due to nominalism, I do not believe we can really comprehend the gravity of this sin. We cannot understand that when we take His name in vain, regardless of our impulsivity and interior freedom, something gravely wrong has taken place. The name of Christ signifies the Godhead to whom we long to know in order to love. It doesn't matter if we have used His name with another self-reported definition—His name has objective meaning and signification. Likewise, when we simply get the *sacraments* done, it takes on a likeness to using God's name in vain.

Sacraments as Necessary For Salvation

We might mention to the bewilderment of the pluralist that these sacraments are necessary to salvation. The term "necessary" is something that ought to be nuanced, but not in such a way that we nuance it out of existence. God is not *merely* offering us a *privileged* path towards salvation, but by His will is ordering a *normative* path to salvation. A *normative* path to salvation is a very different term than a *privileged* path to salvation. "Normative" unveils for us something about the mind of God, His constituted order, and law. Privilege, on the other hand, denotes *grace* and *excellence*. We do not want to generate a dichotomy between grace and the law. God's law is not extrinsic or nominal to man, but rather our participation in his own Divine Essence.[30] But if we do not say that the sacraments are "both," dangerous errors arise. We must hold them both in a radical tension. Let us consider this quote from Pope Paul VI:

> The Church is deeply aware of her duty to preach salvation to all. Knowing that the Gospel message is not reserved to a small group of the initiated, the privileged or the elect, but is destined for everyone, she shares Christ's anguish at the sight of the wandering and exhausted crowds, "like sheep without

---

[30] ST I q 44 a 1.

a shepherd" and she often repeats His words: "I feel sorry for all these people."[31]

Here the Church comes to know Christ more deeply in entering into the vicarious ache of His own heart as He sees man's rational appetite starving. The Church comes to not only will the good of the other in regard to their sensitive appetite, but man's intellectual appetite. In being capable of entering into this dimension of Christ's heart, we come to know more deeply His universal or Catholic approach to salvation. Thus we internalize the Church as one speaking to a woman at the well, thirsting for her faith.

Without grace and the normative laws ordained by God being integrated there will be incredible and ongoing division within the Body of Christ. Jesus may have come to bring the sword, but as one friend of mine says, "He did not come to bring the sword against His own body." If we stress one to the disparaging of the other, we tend to foster a pluralism or a legalism. I submit that the solution is to (1) understand the relational dimension that becomes the integrative principle in these two concepts of grace (privilege) and law (norms/order); and (2) that as a Church we truly internalize God as the first cause, and His essence, by grace is what we are destined to seek. When we understand God as the first cause, we always have a necessary connection (relationally) between the effects of His works with Him as the object of our worship. This rightly ordered relationship helps us internalize what comes from God, ultimately returns

---

[31] Pope Paul VI, *Evangelii Nuntiandi*, 57. Online at https://www.vatican.va/

us to Him. This is the proper disposition of the faith, which thereby enables us to truly *return* to Christ or to love Him in worship.

PART IV

THE RECIPROCITY OF FAITH AND SACRAMENT

Amen, amen dico vobis: qui credit in me, habet vitam aeternam.

"Amen, amen I say to you: he who believes in me has eternal life."

John 6:46

Perhaps the best illustration is where Christ stresses in John 6 that faith is necessary for salvation. He also stresses that eating His flesh is necessary for salvation. Yet it would seem that it easily occurs that these two statements are somehow perceived to be substantially different. They are not, because the object of them is the Son of God.

In order to demonstrate that these two dimensions, the necessity of the Eucharist for salvation and faith are reciprocal, I would like to examine two quotes from St. Thomas Aquinas' commentary.

> "...with faith made living by love, which not only perfects the intellect but the affections as well (for we do not tend to things we believe unless we love them), has eternal life.... So he who believes in Christ so that he tends to him, possesses Christ in his affections and in his intellect. And if we add that Christ is eternal life, as stated *in that we may be in his true Son, Jesus*

Christ. This is the true God and eternal life... we can
infer that whoever believes in Christ has eternal life." [32]

Once again, in this quote we discover that faith involves the *whole person* assenting to God: body, mind and soul. This movement of faith is an active dimension within man, not something passive. In this way, faith is a virtue, not a belief that is imposed upon us against our will and has no connection to the movement of the will. Furthermore, Aquinas addresses both the affectual type of love, as well as that which arises from knowledge in regard to will. This reality of salvation therefore becomes the unity of our appetites with Christ, the fulfillment of all desire. We will ask ourselves here a few questions: What is the object of our faith? Christ. What is the Eucharist? Christ. What is the designated-intrinsic act of reception of the Eucharist? A non-nominal communion with Christ.

We might say therefore, that faith is a general term, but reception of the Eucharist is a particular incarnation of faith. The term, which points toward the Substance of Christ, likewise is discovered substantially in the Eucharist.

"This reality of the sacrament is twofold: one is contained and signified, and this is the whole Christ, who is contained under the species of bread and wine. The other reality is signified but not contained, and this is the mystical body of Christ, which is in the predestined, the called, and the justified. Thus, in reference to Christ as contained and signified,

---

[32] St. Thomas Aquinas, *Commentary on John*, Lecture 6, #950.

one eats his flesh and drinks his blood in a spiritual way if he is united to him through faith and love, so that one is transformed into him and becomes his member: for this food is not changed into the one who eats it, but it turns the one who takes it into itself, as we see in Augustine, when he says: *I am the food of the robust. Grow and you will eat me. Yet you will not change me into yourself, but you will be transformed into me.*"[33]

Here, St. Thomas understands that the reception of the Eucharist is not a mere hoop to jump through, but that internally there is faith which joins us in communion with God. As is the case in our embodied spirits, things are not abstractly participated in, as though our soul dualistically finds nourishment without the body. Such would be a type of Gnosticism that Pope Francis seems to stress is reemerging.[34] Rather, the movement of the will to be united to Christ takes place in the act of a sacramental *receptivity*. In this we operate our body not merely in a signifying nominal manner, but in the very reality of union itself. And it is for this reason that Christ uses the same phraseology to explain that salvation in the gnawing on the Eucharist and through faith are not substantially different in their object.

But if we approach the analogical fridge-door of our soul with a nominal understanding of the sacraments or a type of extrinsic-

[33] St. Thomas Aquinas, *Commentary on John*, Lecture 6, #972.

[34] Pope Francis, *Gaudete et Exsultate*, 36-46. Online at https://www.vatican.va/

dialectic, the assimilating dimension (fruitfulness) of reception of the Eucharist cannot take place. Knowledge which is merely extrinsic is sometimes referred to as a merely abstract approach to spirituality and God. Such abstraction, rationalism, or extrinsic-dialectical thinking is devoid of the type of knowledge that is relational with God. When scripture uses the term "know" in an intimate context, it contains the type of knowledge Aquinas spoke about which differs from the mere "book-smarts" of what people mean by knowledge today. Consider the words of Pope Francis: "Only the action of the Spirit can bring to completion our knowledge of the mystery of God, for the mystery of God is not a question of something grasped mentally but a relationship that touches all of life."[35] In this sense, one cannot really speak of knowledge without its intrinsic connection to love when examining the intellectual appetite of Aquinas. Pope Francis continues by saying: "...in the same journey of knowledge of the mystery of God... is the mystery of love." Abstract knowledge, rationalism, and gnostic mindsets tend to enable man to compartmentalize one's way of life, generating a double-life. In as much as man exercises time and thought on one subject, he then flips to the next subject without integration or practical assimilation. In this sense man acts according to his current speculation, but never develops the practical interior virtues that cause Him to become Christ in the concrete. In this way man never becomes what he consumes, because that which is abstract remains abstract and un-incarnational. "The full extent of our formation is our conformation to

---

[35] Pope Francis, *Desiderio Desideravi*, pp 39. Online at https://www.vatican.va/

Christ. I repeat: it does not have to do with an abstract mental process, but with becoming Him."[36] Therefore, with nominal faith, our
worship at Mass gaslights others in regard to our interior life, as well
as the very essence and meaning of worship in the liturgy. In as
much as one can be a member of the visible Church, so can one
through the absence of charity be separated from the mystical dimension of the Church. Knowledge that is disconnected from symbolic activity in the body and genuine movements of the will is precisely what I mean by an extrinsic-dialectic here. There is nothing
integrated, second-nature, or practically evident in man's relationship with God when such knowledge exists at such a superficial level.
Failure to internalize such precepts through the gift of the Spirit
leads to a type of worship that is vacuous and disinterested, or,
worse, for the sake of some ideological agenda. Within the extrinsic-
dialectic approach to union with the Logos there is a checklist in regard to external behavior. Within the nominal approach to faith
there is a disembodied non-sacramental approach to faith. In this
way, an extrinsic dialectic does not plunge man into the very mystery of God, but rather keeps him *about God*. In this sense, the extrinsic dialectic approach to knowledge becomes another type of
nominalism. Contrary to all of this we find in the Gospel of John
chapter 6 there is *gnawing* and *faith*, integrated.

Without an explicit awareness of our hunger for Christ, and the
internalization of Christ Himself as the object of our will, we are
devastatingly incomplete and wayward. Even with a type of anonymous or nominal experience of the Lord, our intellectual appetite

---

[36] Ibid., 41.

does not find clear direction toward final rest. On this point, man has a natural type of *erotic* desire for the truth which sometimes has been called veracity.[37] This disposition within man is not a matter of willing, but is an ontological configuration. We are ontologically configured to know truth *intrinsically*, and to declare it explicitly. Therefore if we are to address evangelization without anonymity nor as mere extrinsic content, we are being true to our good nature. From a relationship point of view, a good mother and father do not want to know their children vaguely. Rather, they want to know them deeply, explicitly, through conversation, through unity. Any-one who loves God as the object of their intellect, wants to know Him to the fullest extent possible. By nature, that is God as the first principle, and by grace His essence in the beatific vision, according to Aquinas.

Eucharist as Communion with the Substance of God

Toward the error of radical pluralism that touches on the Church's relationship with other religions, it is so important that what we say lines up with this notion of veracity. If we somehow abandon this dimension of God's good design, we have abandoned our humanity. We must understand that radical pluralism is at odds with not only with our ontological configuration towards the truth, but it is also at odds with a genuine love of God. If we understand the rational appetite as being intrinsically relational, an indifference

---

[37] Robert Sokolowski, *Phenomenology of the Human Person* (Cambridge: Cambridge University Press, 2008), 20-21.

to the ultimate cause of all things that are good is not an option—and it would be insulting to suggest that any religion should be content with that.

We must therefore discern the *object* of the Church's nature to be inclusive or receptive. The object of receptivity for the Catholic Church is Christ. That is to say, Christ is the one we are called to receive, and receive explicitly due to the ontological demands of veracity. Therefore the Church operates as a Bride to Christ, seeking to receive Him, and inviting the whole of humanity to the same activity for their own sake, for the building up of God's kingdom, and for the glory of God. Sometimes, an alternative version of inclusivity is suggested, in that the Church is called to include all people, period. In this incomplete approach, there fails to be the invitation to *include God*. We find ourselves again at a place where an integration has not taken place. The Church is called to be inclusive in the same manner that Christ is, since we obtain to His mission. He points us toward a relationship with His Father, and includes us in this endeavor. But to simply include people, period, is to leave out the ultimate mission of God: communion with the Trinity. Thus, the universal dimension of the Church is subsequent and conditioned by the call to be in communion with God. I believe that this is the only way for us to safeguard the inclusive nature from a mode of mission that actually contradicts Christ's great commission and act of feeding the five thousand. Therefore, I end this chapter by simply asking you, the reader: as you sit at the feet of Christ, amongst the crowd: how will you choose to be fed? What type of faith will enable you to truly be nourished?

When our faith has become nominal, when our encounters with the Lord do not penetrate the whole person, our participation in the Eucharist likewise is nominal. It is therefore important that we address the interior longing of mankind to know God as the Cause of all things. In understanding the relationship between cause and effect on a spiritual level, we therefore understand the personal relationship between Creator and creature, Redeemer and Redeemed, Lover and beloved child. This scientific approach to theology, philosophy, and our faith holds our interpretation of personal experiences of God accountable. The language of these sciences give rise to an intelligent expression of phenomenon experienced in the Christian life, and the Sacraments. These truths need to accompany the subjective dimension of human experience in grace in order to divesting ourselves of a sickly sweet sentimentality that ultimately says nothing, and a rigid fundamentalism that treats God's laws as though there are artificially imposed upon mankind. Without good and proper teaching informing our faith, the Eucharist will not be known, and not be loved. Nor will the very mission by which we are consummate with Christ in the Eucharist be extended to those who go hungry. Our inclusion will be with a broken community displaced from God as the object of its hunger.

When by grace man is inflamed with a desire to know the very essence of God, we move beyond the understanding of God as the first cause of all good things, and come to desire something more intense. This intensity of desire, this appetite for God, presents itself most significantly where the Eucharist truly brings to us the very substance of God Himself. And although that presence is veiled by the appearance of bread, an interior faith enables us to penetrate the truths revealed about "the mystery of faith."[38] This mystery of faith, thus cannot merely be penetrated by the science of philosophy, but the virtue of faith. Such faith needs to be formed by the truth about the Eucharist, and the means by which Christ comes to us. The very impulse of His heart that causes the change in substance at every mass. Does our faith penetrate the very motive of God reaching out to His people? Does faith enable us to realize with our whole body and soul, that we are truly before the moment where Christ was crucified? Are we able to present our whole selves before Christ, the Angels and all the saints in heaven? We cannot love this mystery, if we do not know the mystery. We cannot love Christ in the Eucharist if we do not know Him.

---

[38] St. Paul VI, Mysterium Fidei, pp 1, 16. Online at Vatican.va

Chapter 7

The Eucharist and St. Thérèse of Lisieux's "Little Way"

Chantal LaFortune

St. Thérèse of Lisieux is one of the most popular saints of modern times. Famous for her "Little Way," countless Catholics throughout the past century have found in Thérèse one to whom they can relate on a very personal level, by virtue of her emphasis on attaining sanctity through the very ordinary things of daily life. Lesser known about this great saint, however, is her deep love for Our Lord in the Holy Eucharist. Her perpetual childlike trust in God permeated her love for Him in the Eucharist, giving the faithful a beautiful inspiration for a deeper devotion to the Eucharistic Lord through her autobiography and the many letters that she wrote during her life. St. Thérèse's great love for the Eucharist is at the heart of her "Little Way."

St. Thérèse developed her love for the Eucharist as a young child, thanks to the holy influence of her saintly parents. Louis and Azelie Martin—themselves now canonized saints—encouraged their daughters to receive Holy Communion as often as possible. At that time, the faithful were only permitted to receive Communion on major feasts, rather than every Sunday; it was not until the pontificate of Pope St. Pius X that Catholics were universally permitted to receive Holy Communion daily.[1] However, Louis and Azelie Martin attended daily Mass and received Communion as often as they were permitted, and their daughters later wrote that the couple received Communion more frequently than most Catholics at that time. Louis and Azelie also observed the First Friday devotion, receiving Holy Communion every First Friday in accordance with the promises Our Lord made to St. Margaret Mary Alacoque. Even just a few weeks before her death, Azelie went to Mass and received Holy Communion on the First Friday of the month, despite being so weak from stage IV breast cancer that she did not even have the strength to open the church door by herself.[2] Her parents' great devotion to the Eucharist had a profound impact on little Thérèse.

Being a sensitive child, young Thérèse quickly developed her own love for Jesus in the Eucharist. In 1876, Azelie wrote the following about an exchange between three-year-old Thérèse and her next older sister, Celine:

Celine asked the other day: "How can God get into such a little Host?" Therese answered her: "It's not surprising, since Our Lord is almighty." "What does almighty mean?" "It means He can do whatever He wants."[3]

---

[1] Therese Martin, *The Story of a Soul,* trans. Michael Day (Charlotte: TAN, 2010), 44; Thomas Scannel, "Frequent Communion," in *The Catholic Encyclopedia*, Vol. 6 (New York: Robert Appleton Company, 1909). Online at https://www.newadvent.org/cathen/06278a.htm

[2] Patrick O'Hearn, *Parents of the Saints: The Hidden Heroes Behind Our Favorite Saints* (Gastonia, NC: TAN, 2020), Part I, Sts. Louis and Zélie Martin and Pierre Martin, eBook.

[3] Martin, *The Story of a Soul,* 11.

After Azelie's death, Louis and Thérèse would walk to a different church each day to pray before the Blessed Sacrament, trips which Thérèse later recalled with fondness. As a young girl, Thérèse loved to throw rose petals before Eucharistic processions, taking great delight whenever one of her petals touched the Monstrance. Therese looked forward to attending High Mass with her family each Sunday, even before she was old enough to receive Holy Communion herself. The best moments of Thérèse's childhood centered around the Eucharist, a fact which would continue throughout her entire life.

As a child, Thérèse longed for the day when she could receive her First Communion. When Celine was preparing for hers, Thérèse would try to listen to her lessons with Pauline but was told that she was too young. This greatly saddened young Thérèse, who thought, "Surely… four years was not too long to spend preparing to receive Our Lord." Upon hearing Pauline instructing Celine that she "must begin an entirely new life" after receiving her First Communion, Thérèse resolved in her heart to begin this new life at the same time as Celine, rather than waiting for her own.[4] Thus, Thérèse spent most of her childhood preparing for her First Communion. During the last three months leading up to this day, she entered a period of intense spiritual preparation under the guidance and direction of her older sister, Marie. Thérèse set about making "many sacrifices and acts of love," which she said "were transformed into flowers.… I wanted all the flowers on earth to cradle Jesus in my heart."[5]

---

[4] Ibid., 31.
[5] Ibid., 41.

Pauline, who had already entered Carmel at this time, gave Therese a notebook in which to keep count of all her prayers and sacrifices as she prepared for her First Communion. In the duration of just three months, Thérèse recorded "818 sacrifices and 2,773 acts of love or aspirations."[6]

Thérèse called the day on which she received her First Holy Communion "the most wonderful day of my life," so ecstatic was she after waiting eleven long years for this day.[7] Her First Communion remained extraordinarily vivid in Thérèse's memory for her entire life. In describing the moment in her autobiography, the Little Flower wrote:

> How lovely it was, that first kiss of Jesus in my heart—it was truly a kiss of love. I knew that I was loved and said, "I love You and I give myself to You forever." … [I]t was a complete fusion. We were no longer two, for Therese had disappeared like a drop of water lost in the mighty ocean. Jesus alone remained—the Master and the king. … It was joy alone, deep ineffable joy that filled my heart.[8]

So overcome with joy was she upon receiving Our Lord in Holy Communion that Thérèse began to weep. That evening, Thérèse and her father went to the Carmelite convent to see Pauline take the veil.

---

[6] Pauline Martin, "Agnes of Jesus, O.C.D." in *St. Therese of Lisieux by Those Who Knew Her*, trans. Christopher O'Mahony (Huntington, IN: Our Sunday Visitor, 1978), 24.

[7] Ibid., 43.

[8] Martin, *The Story of a Soul,* 43-44.

Pauline noted that her littlest sister looked like "a seraph[,] … like someone who no longer lived on this earth."[9] Marie, too, thought that Thérèse seemed to be "an angel rather than a mortal creature" on the day of her First Communion.[10] Thérèse received her First Communion with an uncommonly heavenly ecstasy.

Her First Communion marked a turning point in Thérèse's life. She had always been an extraordinarily pious and virtuous child, but her love for God greatly increased after her First Communion. Marcelline-Anne Husé, the governess of Thérèse's cousins, with whom Thérèse often played, later wrote:

[S]ince her first [C]ommunion I saw Therese grow in grace and virtue in a very remarkable manner…. One felt about her that she was a person who always lived in God's presence, because if one spoke to her of little matters of female vanity there was no holding her attention for very long, but when I talked with her on pious subjects, she immediately opened up and her heart overflowed with happiness.[11]

Thérèse's "soul aspired with all its strength to be united to Jesus," and this longing only increased after the reception of her first Holy Communion.[12] Despite being surrounded by pretty dresses and

---

[9] Martin, "Agnes of Jesus, O.C.D.," 44.

[10] Marie Martin, "Marie of the Sacred Heart, O.C.D." in *St. Therese of Lisieux by Those Who Knew Her*, 88.

[11] Marcelline-Anne Husé, "Marie-Joseph of the Cross, O.S.B." in *St. Therese of Lisieux by Those Who Knew Her*, 188-189.

[12] Ibid., 88.

many gifts in honor of the occasion, Thérèse felt "a veil of melancholy" the next day; nothing on earth could fill the longing in her heart for the physical union with Our Lord in the Holy Eucharist. The second time she was able to receive Communion was a few weeks later, on Ascension Thursday; she was again overwhelmed with "indescribable joy" and wept upon receiving Communion.[13] Acutely aware of the union between God and man in the reception of Holy Communion, she knew that the words of St. Paul had been fulfilled in her: "And I live, now not I; but Christ liveth in me" (Galatians 2:20 DRB).

Her burning desire to receive Jesus in Holy Communion remained in Thérèse's heart right up until her death. It was the only desire of her heart, beautifully articulated in the last poem she wrote before her death:

> You who know my extreme littleness, / You who aren't afraid to lower yourself to me! / Come into my heart, O white Host that I love, / Come into my heart, it longs for you! / Ah! I wish that your goodness / Would let me die of love after this favor. / Jesus! Hear the cry of my affection. / Come into my heart![14]

---

[13] Martin, *The Story of a Soul,* 44.

[14] Therese Martin, "You Who Know My Extreme Littleness," Archives du Carmel de Lisieux, Washington Province of Discalced Carmelite Friars, Inc, July 1897. Online at https://www.archives-carmel-lisieux.fr/english/carmel/index.php/ps-8

When Thérèse entered Carmel at the age of fifteen, she was dismayed to learn that the Mother Superior did not allow the nuns to receive Communion daily. This "pained [Thérèse] deeply," and she never ceased to pray that one day, the nuns at Carmel would be permitted to receive daily Communion, a prayer that was answered just weeks after her death.[15] In 1891, influenza swept through the Carmel of Lisieux, and many of the nuns became seriously ill or died. During this difficult time, Thérèse was given the role of sacristan, and she took great joy in being able to handle the sacred vessels and altar linens. She felt a responsibility to be even more reverent toward the Eucharist, recalling the words from the Ordination Mass of a Deacon: "'Be ye holy, ye who carry the vessels of the Lord.'"[16]

During the influenza epidemic, Thérèse was also permitted to receive Holy Communion daily, a blessing which filled her with great joy. However, Thérèse admitted that her time of thanksgiving after receiving Holy Communion was often filled with distraction and devoid of any consolation. She would frequently become drowsy during her thanksgiving, but rather than resign herself to an imperfect thanksgiving, she would subsequently spend the rest of the day making a thanksgiving in her heart. Thérèse never became perturbed by her lack of consolation after receiving Communion, saying, "I desire Him to come for His own pleasure, not for mine."[17]

---

[15] Julia-Marie-Elisa Leroyer, "Teresa of Saint Augustine, O.C.D." in *St. Therese of Lisieux by Those Who Knew Her*, 191.

[16] Martin, *The Story of a Soul*, 104.

[17] Ibid., 104.

Though she humbly recognized her great unworthiness to receive the inestimable blessing of the Eucharist, Thérèse never ceased to turn to Our Lady with childlike trust, asking the Blessed Mother to prepare her heart so that Our Lord could come to her and that all of Heaven may glorify Him through her little heart. In 1889, when Thérèse learned that her cousin Marie had been abstaining from receiving Communion out of a scrupulous fear of sacrilege, Thérèse wrote a long, beautiful letter exhorting her cousin to never allow scruples to keep her from receiving Holy Communion. Thérèse said that such fears were from the devil:

> The evil one knows well that he can't make a soul that wants to belong totally to Jesus commit a sin, so he tries to make the soul believe it has.… [H]e wants to deprive Jesus of a loved tabernacle, and, not being able to enter this sanctuary, he wants, at least, that it remain empty and without any Master! When the devil has succeeded in drawing the soul away from Holy Communion, he has won everything.… And Jesus weeps! [18]

Thérèse told Marie that she keenly understood her sufferings, having struggled with severe scruples herself. Thérèse said that the best remedy to overcome the devil's wiles in making a soul scrupu-

---

[18] Therese Martin, "To Marie Guerin – May 30, 1889," Archives du Carmel de Lisieux, Washington Province of Discalced Carmelite Friars, Inc, May 30, 1889. Online at https://www.archives-carmel-lisieux.fr/english/carmel/index.php/mai-1889/11284-lt-92-a-marie-guerin

lous is to receive Our Lord in Holy Communion very frequently, thereby frustrating the enemy's plans.

Thérèse's reference to the soul as a tabernacle reveals the heart of her Eucharistic spirituality. Best expressed in her poem "My Desires Near Jesus Hidden in His Prison of Love," Thérèse desired to become so closely united with the Eucharist that her very soul would become a tabernacle: "He comes within me; by his presence I am a living Monstrance!" She longed for Jesus to "transform" her into His very self.[19] With her characteristic childlike trust, she begged God to live in her forever—even between her physical receptions of Holy Communion—so that she could be a tabernacle housing her Divine Spouse within herself. In return for this great favor, Thérèse offered herself as a victim of God's merciful love, asking that He allow His love to consume her and enflame her heart with love, thereby transforming it to be one with His. This Oblation to Merciful Love had a profound impact on Thérèse's fellow sisters at Carmel, who later spoke with great awe of her offering and desire to be a living tabernacle housing Jesus Christ. Thérèse recognized in the Eucharist the manifestation of God's eternal love for His children, and she desired to be consumed by this love.

St. Thérèse's great love for the Eucharist serves as a powerful example of the kind of devotion all Catholics should have toward the Eucharist. The basis of her "Little Way" is to become like a child in

---

[19] Therese Martin, "My Desires Near Jesus Hidden in His Prison of Love," Archives du Carmel de Lisieux, Washington Province of Discalced Carmelite Friars, Inc, 1895. Online at https://www.archives-carmel-lisieux.fr/english/carmel/index.php/pn-25

one's relationship with God, and this aptly summarizes St. Thérèse's approach to the Eucharist as well. Her parents' strong devotion to the Eucharist planted the seeds of Thérèse's own love for the Sacrament, a love which blossomed into a life-long ardent devotion. Her long preparation for the reception of her First Communion was spent not only studying theology but also living the faith through frequent acts of love and many small sacrifices offered for love of God. Her First Communion marked a turning point in Thérèse's life, after which she had an even more fervent love for God. The greatest desire of her heart was always to receive Our Lord again in Holy Communion, and it was a great sorrow to her when she was not permitted to receive Communion daily. Despite rarely feeling any consolation during her thanksgivings after receiving Holy Communion, St. Thérèse's heart was so filled with love for God that she did not allow herself to become dejected but rather humbly accepted this as a sign of God's unending love for her. She recognized her unworthiness to receive the King of Kings and, with childlike trust, abandoned herself to God's mercy through His Mother. She longed for Jesus to transform her into a living tabernacle, residing in her heart forever and immolating it with His love. The life and writings of St. Thérèse of Lisieux show how the Eucharist is truly the Sacrament of love, an intimate union between the human soul and its Creator, Who desires the love of each soul. May the example of the Little Flower inspire the faithful to cultivate an ever deeper love for Our Lord in the Holy Eucharist, recognizing in this Sacrament the enduring manifestation of God's unending love for His children.

Chapter 8

The One Great Thing to Love on Earth:
J.R.R. Tolkien on the Eucharist

Kaleb Hammond

J.R.R. Tolkien is one of the most beloved authors of all time. Famous for his works of fantasy literature, particularly *The Hobbit* and *The Lord of the Rings*, Tolkien has more recently entered the mainstream of popular culture due to the success of the film adaptations of his books by Peter Jackson. Although Tolkien died in 1973, his continued admiration by literary scholars and casual readers alike has also inspired writers such as Joseph Pearce, Peter Kreeft, and Bradley Birzer to investigate Tolkien's personal life, the influences which inspired his writing and his relationships with other contemporary authors, such as C.S. Lewis. These investigations, however, are not only the result of professional or even literary interest, but are frequently motivated by another, more profound desire: to discover the source from which Tolkien drew out the spiritual meaning and insight underlying the whole of his fictional Middle-earth, what Fleming Rutledge has called a kind of "parallel narrative" being told simultaneous with the apparent story through its symbolism, subtle dialogue references, and character analogues.[1]

---

[1] Fleming Rutledge, *The Battle for Middle-earth* (Grand Rapids, MI: Eerdmans, 2004), 2.

All of this has led the aforementioned writers and many others to realize, especially through the study of Tolkien's private correspondence and nonfiction works, that he was a devout Catholic whose faith, rooted and nourished within the cultural soil and revelatory light of the Church, was the primary inspiration for his writings. On no other point is this connection more apparent than the Blessed Sacrament of the Eucharist, for which Tolkien possessed a lifelong, passionate devotion. Most of all, he believed in the evangelical power of beauty, and it was with great beauty that he expressed his adoration of the Eucharist.

The seeds of Tolkien's Catholic faith were planted by his mother, who, soon after her husband Arthur's untimely death in South Africa and her return to England with her two sons, converted to Catholicism. Tolkien would always consider her to be a martyr for the Faith due to the loyalty to the Church which she displayed during his childhood while suffering and eventually dying from diabetes (largely untreatable at the time) and the abandonment of her anti-Catholic relatives, inspiring him for the rest of his life.[2] Tolkien and his brother Hilary were then raised by Fr. Francis Morgan, a priest of the Birmingham Oratory founded by St. John Henry Newman, and spent much of their time around the priests, with Tolkien later writing that he was "virtually a junior inmate" of the Oratory and that he and his brother served Mass with the fathers daily,[3] cultivating a love for the Eucharist diffused from his priest-guardian and the

---

[2] J.R.R. Tolkien; Humphrey Carpenter and Christopher Tolkien (eds), *The Letters of J.R.R. Tolkien* (New York: Houghton Mifflin, 2000), 340, 353. Kindle.

[3] Ibid., 394.

spirituality of the Oratory. He even expressed his enjoyment of High Mass to his future wife, Edith Bratt, whom he helped convert to the Faith prior to their marriage.[4]

After becoming an Oxford don and serving in the Great War, Tolkien passed on his inherited Catholic faith to his children, to whom he regularly instilled his devotion to and love of the Eucharist. Tolkien wrote to his son Michael that "I fell in love with the Blessed Sacrament from the beginning— –and by the mercy of God never have fallen out again," yet even when he struggled with his faith as a young man, the Eucharist was the persistent force which called him home: "Not for me the Hound of Heaven, but the never-ceasing silent appeal of Tabernacle, and the sense of starving hunger." For this reason, he counselled Michael to always cling to the Blessed Sacrament whenever he experienced similar difficulties in his spiritual life:

> The only cure for sagging [or] fainting faith is Communion. Though always Itself, perfect and complete and inviolate, the Blessed Sacrament does not operate completely and once for all in any of us. Like the act of Faith it must be continuous and grow by exercise. Frequency is of the highest effect.[5]

He also gave similar advice to his son Christopher:

---

[4] Ibid., 7.
[5] Ibid., 338.

If you don't do so already, make a habit of the 'praises'. I use them much (in Latin): the Gloria Patri, the Gloria in Excelsis, the Laudate Dominum; the Laudate Pueri Dominum (of which I am specially fond), one of the Sunday psalms; and the Magnificat; also the Litany of Loretto (with the prayer Sub tuum praesidium). If you have these by heart you never need for words of joy. It is also a good and admirable thing to know by heart the Canon of the Mass, for you can say this in your heart if ever hard circumstance keeps you from hearing Mass.[6]

Tolkien once described to Christopher a vision he experienced while attending the *Quarant' Ore* Forty Hours devotion before the Blessed Sacrament:

I perceived or thought of the Light of God and in it suspended one small mote (or millions of motes to only one of which was my small mind directed), glittering white because of the individual ray from the Light which both held and lit it…. And the ray was the Guardian Angel of the mote: not a thing interposed between God and the creature, but God's very attention itself, personalized…. the shining poised mote was myself (or any other human person that I might think of with love)…. As the love of the Father and Son (who are infinite and equal) is a Person, so the love and attention of the

---

[6] Ibid., 66.

Light to the Mote is a person (that is both with us and in Heaven): finite but divine: i.e. angelic.[7]

Like many other saints in history, Tolkien's vision was directly tied to the Eucharist, with the grace of God communicated through Tolkien's faith and wisdom providing an insight into the nature of the love of God and of angels as the heavenly messengers of his love. Tolkien wrote that this vision "was very immediate, and not recapturable in clumsy language, certainly not the great sense of joy that accompanied it",[8] an epiphany of beauty experienced as a kind of reward for his lifelong love of the Eucharist. Even in the midst of personal struggles, the difficulties of his writing and his work as an Oxford professor, helping his wife with her health issues and seeing two of his sons go off to fight in the Second World War (though his eldest son, John, was ordained a Catholic priest just after the war in 1946), he remained a daily communicant,[9] serving at Mass as an adult[10] and never failing to boldly proclaim his Catholic faith even amidst anti-Catholic prejudice from some of his friends and coworkers, including C.S. Lewis.[11]

In another letter to Michael, giving advice on marriage and relationships, Tolkien composed one of the most profound and poetic

---

[7] Ibid., 99.

[8] Ibid., 99.

[9] George W. Rutler, "To his dying day, Tolkien was a daily communicant," Catholic Education Resource Center (19 May 2019). Online at https://www.catholiceducation.org.

[10] Tolkien, *The Letters of J.R.R. Tolkien*, 115.

[11] Ibid., 96.

testimonies to the Eucharist in history, employing the languages of epic literature and Catholic theology with which he was intimately versed:

> Out of the darkness of my life, so much frustrated, I put before you the one great thing to love on earth: the Blessed Sacrament…. There you will find romance, glory, honour, fidelity, and the true way of all your loves upon earth, and more than that: Death: by the divine paradox, that which ends life, and demands the surrender of all, and yet by the taste (or foretaste) of which alone can what you seek in your earthly relationships (love, faithfulness, joy) be maintained, or take on that complexion of reality, of eternal endurance, which every man's heart desires.[12]

Later in Tolkien's life, during the 1960s and just before his death in 1973, Tolkien was faced with the many changes occurring in the Church, particularly as a result of the Second Vatican Council and the Mass of St. Paul VI. Like many of his time, including Evelyn Waugh and Joseph Ratzinger, as well as those today, Tolkien struggled with the plethora of abuses that rabidly fungated in the new Mass, often in violation of Vatican II and of the Church's two-thousand-year liturgical tradition. He wrote to Michael in 1968, "I know quite well that, to you as to me, the Church which once felt like a refuge, now often feels like a trap." In the same letter he expressed his criticism of the trend in doctrinal and liturgical primitivism

---

[12] Ibid., 53-54.

popular at the time, as well as the dangers of the Council's emphases on *aggiornamento* and what he called "ecumenicalness" while stating his belief in the need for ecumenical charity and his admiration for many non-Catholic Christians.[13] This authentic ecumenism also inspired him to join "a combined Christian Council of all denominations" in Oxford and united to fifty other cities.[14]

Tolkien was especially critical of the arbitrary abandonment of Latin, the reduced use of genuflection, and other disciplinary changes in the new Mass, which he, like others, recognized as ultimately false, expressive of the so-called "Spirit of Vatican II" which Pope Benedict XVI has called "a hermeneutic of discontinuity and rupture."[15] Nevertheless, as Tolkien explained, "I think there is nothing to do but to pray, for the Church, the Vicar of Christ, and for ourselves; and meanwhile to exercise the virtue of loyalty, which indeed only becomes a virtue when one is under pressure to desert it."[16] Exhibiting this virtue to a profound degree, like his mother, Tolkien never abandoned his faith, since, as he wrote, even with all the scandals and abuses in the Church, to deny the Eucharist would be to "call Our Lord a fraud to His face."[17] Instead, as he once wrote in answer to Camilla, the young daughter of his publicist Rayner Unwin, "it may be said that the chief purpose of life, for any one of us, is to increase according to our capacity our knowledge of God by

---

[13]Ibid., 393-394.

[14] Ibid., 72.

[15] Pope Benedict XVI, *Vatican II: The Essential Texts* (New York: Image, 2012), 4.

[16] Tolkien, *The Letters of J.R.R. Tolkien*, 393.

[17] Ibid., 337.

all the means we have, and to be moved by it to praise and thanks."[18] As a man educated in history and living in an England which had once been Catholic but had not been so for some four centuries, Tolkien recognized the Catholic Church, led by the Pope, as the greatest champion of the Eucharist, and he saw this fact as its clearest vindication:

> But for me that Church of which the Pope is the acknowledged head on earth has as chief claim that it is the one that has (and still does) ever defended the Blessed Sacrament, and given it most honour, and put it (as Christ plainly intended) in the prime place. 'Feed my sheep' was His last charge to St Peter; and since His words are always first to be understood literally, I suppose them to refer primarily to the Bread of Life.[19]

In what some might see as a contradiction to his strong traditionalism and his rejection of many modern innovations in the Church, Tolkien also recommended to Michael that he go to Mass "in circumstances that affront [his] taste," and when confronted with distraction, annoyance, lack of piety in the faithful or mediocrity in the priest, to "[g]o to Communion with them (and pray for them)."[20] In this way, he showed a profound charity which did not violate but rather expressed his integral faith and upholding of tradition.

---

[18] Ibid., 400.

[19] Ibid., 339.

[20] Ibid., 339.

Following from his lifelong devotion to the Eucharist and his great intellectual brilliance, Tolkien gleaned many insights into the mystery of the Blessed Sacrament. In his seminal essay "On Fairy-Stories," Tolkien explained a concept which he elsewhere termed "the ennoblement (or sanctification) of the humble,"[21] whereby ordinary things of daily experience are enchanted, their inherent wonder, beauty, and gratuity highlighted by a fantastical setting or reimagining, recovered from mundane familiarity: "It was in fairy-stories that I first divined the potency of the words, and the wonder of the things, such as stone, and wood, and iron; tree and grass; house and fire; bread and wine."[22] This concept inspired his understanding of the Gospel as a fairy tale, one which, however, is true in the widest sense, both revealing metaphysical truths and occurring factually in history, and as such it is set apart from other fairy tales while also fulfilling their deepest longings, and indeed the longing of all art, namely for the author to enter his own invented world and for the Author of Creation to enter his own story:

> The Gospels contain a fairy-story, or a story of a larger kind which embraces all the essence of fairy-stories.... But this story has entered History and the primary world; the desire and aspiration of sub-creation has been raised to the fulfillment of Creation.[23]

---

[21] Ibid., 237.

[22] J.R.R. Tolkien, "On Fairy-Stories," in *The Tolkien Reader* (Great Britain: George Allen & Unwin Ltd., 1964), 78.

[23] Ibid., 88.

Thus, while bread and wine are seemingly plain and humble, they are revealed by the Eucharist to involve a special cooperation between God and man, with the subcreative art of the latter tending the creations of the former who then ennobles and hallows the new work by transubstantiating it into the Body and Blood of His Son, Jesus Christ, who becomes the Bread of Life (John 6:35) and whose sacrificial offering is a participation in and foretaste of the eschatological Marriage Supper of the Lamb to which all human feasts point (Revelation 19:9).

While Tolkien's more explicit theological insights can be found in his letters and other writings, the most familiar to readers is communicated in his fiction, particularly *The Lord of the Rings*. A masterpiece of epic fantasy, which Tolkien described as being "of course a fundamentally religious and Catholic work" where "the religious element is absorbed into the story and the symbolism," Tolkien's masterpiece is suffused with Catholic imagery and themes, pertaining especially to the Blessed Virgin, described by Tolkien as "upon which all my own small perception of beauty both in majesty and simplicity is founded,"[24] but also to the Eucharist. He implicitly agreed on this observation made by a critic and believed it to be one way by which it could be "deduced" from the text that he is Catholic:

> [O]ne critic (by letter) asserted that the invocations of Elbereth, and the character of Galadriel as directly described (or through the words of Gimli and Sam) were clearly related to Catholic devotion to Mary. Another saw in waybread

---

[24] Tolkien, *The Letters of J.R.R. Tolkien*, 172.

(lembas)=viaticum and the reference to its feeding the *will* (vol. III, p. 213) and being more potent when fasting, a derivation from the Eucharist. (That is: far greater things may colour the mind in dealing with the lesser things of a fairy-story.)[25]

Like viaticum, lembas in Tolkien's elvish language means "bread for the journey," and in another letter Tolkien upheld its religious significance against a film treatment of the story which described it as a "food concentrate."[26] Similarly, like the manna in the desert eaten by the People of God during the Exodus, lembas is a typological sign pointing forward to the Eucharist. As Bradley Birzer explains:

> Indeed, the Elven lembas arguably serves as Tolkien's most explicit symbol of Christianity in *The Lord of the Rings*; it is a representation, though pre-Christian, of the Eucharist. For Tolkien, nothing represented a greater gift from God than the actual Body and Blood of Christ.[27]

The intellectual and imaginative depth of Tolkien's Catholic faith, most of all his devotion to the Blessed Sacrament, infused every aspect of his life; from its fontal source, Tolkien lived a truly

---

[25] Ibid., 288.

[26] Ibid., 274-275.

[27] Bradley J. Birzer, *Sanctifying Myth: Understanding Middle-earth* (Wilmington, Delaware: ISI Books, 2002), 63.

holy and saintly life, joyously sharing his faith with his family, friends and acquaintances. As his friend and assistant Clyde S. Kilby remarked, "I do not recall a single visit I made to Tolkien's home in which the conversation did not at some point fall easily into a discussion of religion, or rather Christianity,"[28] and according to his son Michael, his faith "pervaded all his thinking, beliefs and everything else."[29] He lived out his faith with courage and humility and at all times it was his love of the Lord's gift of himself in the mystery of the Eucharist which nourished his faith, bolstered his hope, and enflamed his charity. From a heart enlightened by the adoration of the Crucified One, Tolkien gave this poignant reminder:

> No man can estimate what is really happening at the present sub specie aeternitatis. All we do know, and that to a large extent by direct experience, is that evil labours with vast power and perpetual success—in vain: preparing always only the soil for unexpected good to sprout in.[30]

---

[28] Clyde S. Kilby, *Tolkien & The Silmarillion* (Wheaton, IL: Harold Shaw Publishers, 1976), 53.

[29] Joseph Pearce, *Tolkien: Man and Myth* (San Francisco: Ignatius Press, 2001), 194.

[30] Tolkien, *The Letters of J.R.R. Tolkien*, 76.

Chapter 9

The Living Bread: Fulton Sheen's Eucharistic Theology

Joseph Tuttle

"He willed to give us the very life we slew;
to give us the very Food we destroyed;
to nourish us with the very Bread we buried
and the very Blood poured forth.
He made our very crime a *happy fault*."

- The Fulton J. Sheen Sunday Missal

In the 1960s, Venerable Fulton J. Sheen lamented what he called the "de-Eucharistization" of the world. What he meant by the statement was that the world was losing its appreciation for the Eucharist. He said, "A decline in reverence for the Eucharist developed in the Church as there was a rejection of the Manna among the Israelites."[1] Our modern world seeks to make everything into objects. People become objects for pleasure and use instead of being seen as sons and daughters of God. Priests and laity were and still are treating the Eucharist as if it were a piece of bread and a cup of wine, mere objects to be treated as such. Thus, the Person of Jesus Christ truly present in the Blessed Sacrament is seen as an object and

---

[1] Fulton J. Sheen, *Those Mysterious Priests* (Staten Island, New York: St. Pauls Press, 2005), 138.

no longer as a Divine Person. Indeed, the Eucharist is not bread and wine and is far greater than bread and wine. The Eucharist is the body and blood, soul and divinity of Jesus Christ.

Fulton Sheen was a great promoter of the Eucharist writing and speaking extensively on the topic. After his ordination to the priesthood, Sheen took a vow to make a Holy Hour every day of his life, a vow he kept to the very last moments of his life as we shall see. It is the purpose then of this essay to examine Sheen's teachings on the Eucharist in order to better help revive and renew devotion, love, and understanding of the what the *Catechism of the Catholic Church* calls the "Source and summit of the Christian life."[2]

John 6 and the Last Supper

Let us begin with Fulton Sheen's teachings on the Eucharist as presented in Sacred Scripture. The clearest teachings on the Eucharist come from the Gospel of John chapter 6, and the Synoptic Gospels' narration of the Last Supper. In John 6, the Jews and many of Jesus' disciples turned away from Him because of what He said, mainly that the Eucharist *is* His body and blood and not *like* His body and blood. This saying was "too hard" for them. Sheen writes on John 6:

> The Eucharist is so essential to our one-ness with Christ that as soon as Our Lord announced It in the Gospel, It began to be the test of fidelity of His followers. First, he lost the masses,

---

[2] CCC, 1324.

for it was too hard a saying and they no longer followed Him. Secondly, He lost some of His disciples: "They walked with Him no more." Third, it split His apostolic band, for Judas is here announced as the betrayer.[3]

Sheen notes that the sacrament of the priesthood is intimately linked with the sacrament of the Eucharist. These sacraments were instituted on the same night. Sheen states that it was Jesus' teaching on the Eucharist that Judas rejected and thereby rejected Jesus Himself:

Many wonder why Judas broke with Our Lord; they think it was only at the end of Our Lord's life, and that it was only love of money that forced the break. Avarice, indeed it was; but the Gospel tells us the astounding story that Judas broke with Our Divine Lord the day He announced the giving of His Flesh for the life of the world.[4]

Sheen also adds that this lack of belief in the Eucharist is not only relevant for Judas but for all priests: "Scripture gives considerable evidence to prove that a priest begins to fail his priesthood when he fails in his love of the Eucharist."[5] Indeed, any person who does not have a strong love and devotion to the Eucharist will begin to fail in

---

[3] Fulton J. Sheen, *Treasure in Clay* (New York: Image Books, 2008), 202.

[4] Ibid., 190.

[5] Ibid., 201-202.

his life and vocation.

Again, Sheen makes it clear that at the Last Supper, Jesus did not mince His words but clearly stated that the Eucharist is His body and blood. In order to help people better understand the Eucharist, Sheen uses the beautiful example of motherhood:

> To every infant at the breast, the mother virtually says: "Take, eat and drink; this is my body and blood." The mother would be untrue if she said, "This represents my body," knowing that it is her body. So too, the Lord would be untrue to fact if He said: "This is not My Body and Blood. It is only a representation or a symbol of it."[6]

The fact that many people walked away from Christ is evidence that what He was saying was something radical. If Jesus had merely meant the Eucharist to be a symbol of Himself, then His followers would not have left.

The Substances of Bread and Wine

At the Last Supper, Jesus used the substances of bread and wine and transformed them into the substance of His body and blood, soul and divinity. One common question regarding the elements used to confect the Eucharist is why did Jesus, and why does the Church, use bread and wine? There are of course, many biblical roots

---

[6] Fulton J. Sheen, *These Are the Sacraments* (Garden City, New York: Image Books, 1964), 79.

and origins of the Eucharist.[7] Sheen offers three aspects as to why Our Lord used bread and wine.

First, in order for bread to be made, it must undergo a passion of sorts. The wheat must be ground and then baked and so forth. So too the grapes used to make the wine must be plucked and crushed and fermented. Sheen writes on the use of bread:

> An unchanging ritual of the Mass is the Breaking of the Bread to remind us, each time we celebrate, that the Lord was 'broken' for our sins as a victim. The Old Testament already foreshadowed Christ's offering of Himself in the bread that was broken, for it was prescribed that the bread that the priest was to offer was to be "cut up into small pieces" (Lev 2:6).... In this, the bread prefigured the condition of the Victim that is symbolized.[8]

Because Jesus had to endure His Passion, the elements that would be changed into His body and blood must also have undergone a passion. The wheat must be ground and the grapes crushed before they can become bread and wine.

Second, Sheen writes that, "[N]o two substances in nature better symbolize unity than bread and wine. As bread is made from a multiplicity of grains of wheat, and wine is made from a multiplicity

---

[7] See Brant Pitre, *Jesus and the Jewish Roots of the Eucharist*.

[8] Fulton J. Sheen, *The Priest is Not His Own* (San Francisco: Ignatius Press, 2004), 23.

of grapes, so the many who believe are one in Christ."[9] The Church is the Mystical Body of Christ made of many members under the headship of Christ. For Sheen then, bread and wine help us to understand the Mystical Body better.

A final reason Sheen offers is that "[T]here are not two substances in nature which have traditionally nourished man than bread and wine. In bringing these elements to the altar, men are equivalently bringing themselves."[10] In the Eucharist, Christ offers Himself to us, and in the elements that are transformed into the Eucharist, we offer ourselves to God.

Holy Communion

For Sheen, there are three major aspects of Holy Communion:

1. Reception of Divine Life
2. Communion with Christ's Death
3. Communion with the Mystical Body of Christ

Reception of Divine Life and Communion with Christ's Death

Sheen writes that, "Communion then is first of all the receiving of divine life, a life to which we are no more entitled than marble is entitled to blooming. It is the pure gift of an all-merciful God who so loves us that he willed to be united with us, not in the bonds of

---

[9] Sheen, *Treasure in Clay*, 400.
[10] Ibid., 400.

flesh, but in the ineffable bonds of the Spirit where love knows no satiety, but only rapture and joy."[11]

Sheen also writes, however, that, "The Eucharist commits us to both life and death."[12] When writing on Holy Communion, that is, the reception of the Eucharist, Sheen writes that there is a twofold nature to it. Holy Communion has an anabolic (nutritional) and catabolic (victimal) side. These cannot be separated. Sheen begins by discussing the anabolic and catabolic sides of nature in order to better understand the supernature of the Eucharist:

> In nature, death is the condition for life. The vegetables we eat at table have to be sacrificed. They must yield life and substance before they can become the sacrament, the holy thing nourishing the body. They must be torn up from their roots and subjected to fire before they can give more abundant life to the flesh. Before the animal in the field can be our meat, it must be subjected to the knife, to the shedding of blood, and to fire. Only then does it become strong sustenance of the body.[13]

Sheen continues to say that Christ, like the plant and animal matter we eat had to undergo death in order to provide us with divine life. In order to be incorporated with Christ's resurrection and

---

[11] *The Fulton J. Sheen Sunday Missal* (New York: Hawthorn Books, INC., 1961), xxii.

[12] Sheen, *The Priest is Not His Own*, 18.

[13] Ibid., 19.

ascension, we too must be incorporated with Christ's death. Catholics are an Easter people, but they should never forget the Good Friday that preceded it.

In Holy Communion, God gives Himself to man, and man, in turn, should give himself back to God. In writing to priests about the laity receiving Communion, Sheen says:

> Do we teach them that they must not only receive Communion, but give too? They may not accept life while giving no sacrifice. The communion rail is a place of exchange. The people give time and receive eternity; they give self-denial and receive life; they give nothingness and receive all. Holy Communion commits each to a closer union not only with Christ's life, but also with His death-to greater detachment from the world, to surrender of luxuries for the sake of the poor, to death of the old Adam for the rebirth in Christ, the new Adam.[14]

When receiving the Eucharist in Holy Communion, we bring ourselves and all that we have and give them to God. In turn, He gives Himself completely to us. If we do not give ourselves to Him in Holy Communion, then God does not force Himself unto us.

It is interesting to note that the blood found on the Shroud of Turin, the Face Cloth of Oviedo, and the miracle of the bleeding Eucharist in Lanciano, Italy, are all blood type AB. Type AB is that of the universal receiver. Many would think that Christ's blood would

---

[14] Ibid., 20.

be that of the universal donor. Even Christ's blood type found through relics and miracles testifies to the fact that we must give ourselves in Holy Communion as Christ gives of Himself to us.

Communion with the Mystical Body of Christ

Sheen points out a third aspect aside from the anabolic and catabolic natures of Holy Communion: Communion and fellowship with the Mystical Body of Christ. At the reception of Holy Communion, all boundaries are broken between people. The student and the professor, the worker and the employer, all receive the same Eucharist. It dissolves all race, nationalities, and status, for those who receive Him worthily are all adopted children of the Father. Sheen writes that:

The Eucharist, therefore, is the Sacrament not only of our personal perfection, but through it, the Sacrament of the perfection of Christ's Mystical Body which is the Church. Equally united to the same Christ, we are more closely bound up with one another, though we be thousands of miles apart, than we would be with people who sit at our dinner table and yet are ignorant of Christ.[15]

When asked what other sacrament can help us to explain the love of the Eucharist in the reception of Holy Communion, Sheen responds:

---

[15] *The Fulton J. Sheen Sunday Missal*, xxiv.

Matrimony. In marriage, husband and wife are two in one flesh; in the Eucharist, the communicant and Christ are two in one Spirit. The peak of love in the flesh is unity; the peak of love in the Spirit is unity. In both cases, there is unity with the beloved, but in the Eucharist, the Beloved is Christ.[16]

Thus, the Eucharist not only binds us to Christ but also to His Mystical Body, the Church.

The Holy Hour

As part of Sheen's methodology, he always emphasized practicing what one preached. One of the major teachings of Sheen's was on the Holy Hour. Sheen defines it as "[a] continuous and unbroken Hour spent in the presence of Our Divine Lord in the Eucharist."[17] The Holy Hour has its origin in Sacred Scripture:

And he came to the disciples and found them sleeping; and he said to Peter, "So, could you not watch with me one hour? Watch and pray that you may not enter into temptation; the spirit indeed is willing, but the flesh is weak."[18]

In the Garden of Gethsemane, Jesus Himself makes a Holy Hour in preparation for His upcoming Passion. He asks the apostles to do

---

[16] Ibid., xxii.

[17] Fulton J. Sheen, *The Holy Hour* (National Council of Catholic Men, 1962-65), 5.

[18] Matt. 26:40-41.

the same. If Jesus needed to make a Holy Hour, and the apostles needed to make one, how much more do we need to make one? Whenever we want to grow in a relationship with someone, we begin by spending time with them. How much time do we spend on social media, watching movies, and hanging out with our friends? Is not God our greatest friend? And can we not watch one hour with Him?

For Sheen, the purpose of the Holy Hour is mental prayer and a personal encounter with Christ. He does not exclude the idea of reciting common prayers like the "Our Father" and "Hail Mary," but emphasizes the importance of mental prayer, of conversation with God during the Holy Hour. In Sheen's day, as in our own, there was a major lack of mental prayer. Sheen uses an analogy of someone in love to describe mental prayer:

> In the human order a person in love is always conscious of the one loved, lives in the presence of the other, resolves to do the will of the other, and regards as his greatest jealousy being outdone in the least advantage of self-giving. Apply this to a soul in love with God, and you have the rudiments of meditation.[19]

Conversations are always a two-way street, meaning that both people in a conversation speak. We speak with God, and He in turn will speak to us. When we begin these conversations, Sheen says we should begin by placing ourselves in the Presence of God. This means one can make a Holy Hour either when the Blessed Sacrament

---

[19] Sheen, *The Holy Hour*, 5.

is exposed during times of Adoration or when the Blessed Sacrament is reposed in the tabernacle. Once we have entered the Presence of God, we may begin our conversation. Sheen warns that we should not "monopolize" the conversation:

> A conversation is an exchange, not a monologue. As the soul willed to draw near God, God wills to draw near the soul. It would be wrong to monopolize the conversation with friends; it is more wrong to do so in our relations with God. We must not do all the talking; we must also be good listeners.[20]

When it comes to the posture of the Holy Hour, many ask how it should be made. Sheen responds that one should make the Holy Hour on their knees (health, age, and fitness permitting). Why such a posture? Kneeling is a way of humility. Sheen writes: "It is best to kneel during the Holy Hour, for it indicates humility, follows the example of Our Lord in the Garden, makes atonement for our failings and is a polite gesture before the King of Kings."[21] By kneeling before our God in the Blessed Sacrament, we humbly submit ourselves to Him. Our pride is melted away like ice on a windshield when the sun hits it at midday.

Many might ask whether the Holy Hour is difficult. Sheen writes, "Sometimes it seemed hard; it might mean having to forgo a social engagement, or rise an hour earlier, but on the whole it has never

---

[20] Ibid., 6.

[21] Sheen, *The Priest is Not His Own*, 247.

been a burden, only a joy."[22]

Sheen suggests that clergy and religious, and even the laity if they are able, to make a daily Holy Hour. If one cannot, depending on their state in life they should try to make a weekly or monthly Holy Hour. We can only have a relationship with God by spending time with Him. The best way to do this is in His Eucharistic Presence for one singular Hour for which He has asked of us. Sheen writes, "Not for an hour of activity did He plead, but for an hour of companionship."[23]

Sheen had a particular fondness for the Holy Hour. When he was ordained to the priesthood in 1919, he made this promise: "I resolved to spend a continuous Holy Hour every day in the presence of Our Lord in the Blessed Sacrament."[24] Sheen kept this promise for over sixty years, to the very end of his life. His body was found in his private chapel in New York bowed over in the presence of the Blessed Sacrament.

Conclusion

How should the Church go about reviving and renewing devotion and love to the Eucharist, to God Himself? I believe, and I think Sheen would agree, that the keystone of Eucharistic revival and renewal, in any age of the Church, will stem from the Holy Hour. Were not the Apostles, Mary Magdalene, and many others

---

[22] Sheen, *Treasure in Clay*, 198.
[23] Ibid., 198.
[24] Ibid., 197.

transformed merely by being in His Presence? We too can be transformed to live heroic lives of virtue for the greater glory of God by making the Holy Hour and responding to Jesus' call, "Could you not watch with me for one hour?"

Prayer After Holy Communion by Fulton J. Sheen

I give myself to thee O Christ. Here is my body. Take it. Here is my blood. Take it. Here is my soul, my will, my energy, my strength, my property, my wealth, all that I have. Take it. Consecrate it. Offer it. Offer it with thyself to the heavenly Father in order that he, looking down on this great sacrifice, may see not only thee, his beloved Son, but also me in thee. Transmute the poor bread of my life into thy divine Life; thrill the wine of my wasted life into thy divine Spirit; unite my broken heart with thy Heart; change my cross into a crucifix. Let not my abandonment and my sorrow and my bereavement go to waste. Gather up the fragments. As the drop of water is absorbed by the wine at the Offertory of the Mass, let my life be absorbed in thine; let my little cross be entwined with the great Cross, so that I may purchase the joys of everlasting happiness in union with Thee.

Consecrate these trials of my life which would go un-rewarded, unless united with thee; transubstantiate me so that, like the bread which is now thy Body, and the wine which is now thy Blood, I too may be wholly thine. I care not if the species remain, or that, like the bread and the wine, I seem to all earthly eyes the same as before. My station in life, my routine duties, my work, my family, all these are but the species of my life which may remain unchanged; but the substance of my life, my soul, my mind, my will, my heart, transubstantiate them, transform them wholly into thy service, so that through me all may know how sweet is the love of Christ. Amen.[25]

---

[25] *The Fulton J. Sheen Sunday Missal,* xx-xxi.

Chapter 10

Love and Responsibility
for, with, and from the Eucharist

Fr. Dominic Rankin

ABBREVIATIONS

cfr. "conferatur" – meaning "compare to", indicating a reference which is being paraphrased or referenced without being quoted outright.

n. "number" – indicating a paragraph number within a work if it is numbered by paragraph instead of page.

n.b. "nota bene" – meaning "note well", indicating a point to be taken account of, often of information that will continue to apply throughout the paper.

p. "page" – shorthand within citations when indicating a page number in the original source.

Now his parents went to Jerusalem every year at the Feast of the Passover. And when he was twelve years old, they went up according to custom. And when the feast was ended, as they were returning, the boy Jesus stayed behind in Jerusalem. His parents did not know it, but supposing him to be in the group they went a day's journey, but then they began to search for him among their relatives and acquaintances, and when they did not find him, they returned to Jerusalem, searching for him. After three days they found him in the temple, sitting among the teachers, listening to them and asking them questions. And all who heard him were amazed at his understanding and his answers. And when his parents saw him, they were astonished. And his mother said to him, "Son, why have you treated us so? Behold, your father and I have been searching for you in great distress." And he said to them, "Why were you looking for me? Did you not know that I must be in my Father's house?" And they did not understand the saying that he spoke to them. And he went down with them and came to Nazareth and was submissive to them. And his mother treasured up all these things in her heart. And Jesus increased in wisdom and in stature and in favor with God and man.[1]

This essay is a search. Less audacious than Pope Benedict's "personal search 'for the face of the Lord,'"[2] but a search nonetheless for Jesus. I take as my guide Pope St. John Paul II, and my prayer specifically is that he would lead us to Our Lord in the Eucharist, how to abide in holy communion through Christ, with the Heavenly Father. Of course, as soon as that earnest prayer is finished and we get down to examining what the great pope says about the Eucharist, we confront the vastness of the enterprise. Just as Mary and Joseph returning to look for Jesus in Jerusalem must have been awed by the

---

[1] Luke 2:41-54, ESVCE.
[2] Pope Benedict XVI, *Jesus of Nazareth* (New York: Doubleday, 2007), xxiii.

countless places where the Lord could be found, so also we are overwhelmed by the immensity of Pope St. John Paul II's teachings on the Eucharist. One could begin from the obvious place and turn to his final encyclical, *Ecclesia de Eucharistia* of 2003, discovering in those words a summary of his understanding of this sacrament—specifically the relationship between the Eucharistic body of Christ and His Ecclesial body—and in this way a capstone to much of the work and efforts of his pontificate:

> Every commitment to holiness, every activity aimed at carrying out the Church's mission, every work of pastoral planning, must draw the strength it needs from the Eucharistic mystery and in turn be directed to that mystery as its culmination. In the Eucharist we have Jesus, we have his redemptive sacrifice, we have his resurrection, we have the gift of the Holy Spirit, we have adoration, obedience and love of the Father. Were we to disregard the Eucharist, how could we overcome our own deficiency?[3]

On the other end of things, one could perhaps look at the beginning of his pontificate, recalling his Holy Thursday letter of 1980 addressing the mystery and worship of the Holy Eucharist.[4] The avid seeker could continue this exploration and turn to the other letters, as well

---

[3] John Paul II, *Ecclesia de Eucharistia* (Vatican City: Libreria Editrice Vaticana, 2003), n. 60.

[4] Cfr. John Paul II, "Apostolic Letter, Dominicae Cenae," February 24, 1980. Online at https://www.vatican.va/

as homilies, audiences, and angelus addresses of Pope John Paul II's pontificate and find thousands of different occasions where John Paul spoke on the Eucharist in reference to innumerable different situations and directing his words to every possible human group around the planet. Perhaps inspired by that image, the seeker could go all in on the personalistic-approach, looking for stories and anecdotes and particular encounters from the life of the great pope that illustrate his love and understanding for the Blessed Sacrament. Jason Evert has done this vividly in his book *Saint John Paul the Great: His Five Loves*, arguing from countless loving encounters between the Holy Father and the Blessed Sacrament, that truly there we find the heart of the Polish Pope.[5] I make mention here of one memorable moment during one of JPII's visits to the United States:

> ...he [the papal trip-planner, Fr. Tucci] noticed that one of the doors in the hallway the Pope would pass through opened into a chapel with the Blessed Sacrament. He instructed Father White, "Keep that door closed so he doesn't know there's a chapel in there." Upon the Pope's arrival, the door was closed, and John Paul took some time to eat and rest at the residence. When it was time to leave, he walked down the hall, which was lined with doors leading into various rooms, passed by the door of the chapel, then suddenly stopped. He looked back at the door, then looked over at Father Tucci, and without saying a word, wagged his finger at

---

[5] Cfr. Jason Evert, *John Paul the Great: His Five Loves* (Lakewood, CO: Totus Tuus Press, 2014), 130-142.

Chapter 10: Love and Responsibility for, with, and from the Eucharist 201

him and shook his head. Father White recalled: He's never been in this place before, never set eyes on the place, and there was nothing about the door that distinguished it in any way as a chapel. It was just one more door in a corridor of doors. But he turned right back around, he opened that door up, and he went into the chapel and he prayed. According to Father White, the Holy Father remained in prayer long enough to "do some damage" to the schedule, then left the residence to head to his appointment.[6]

A close friend of the Holy Father, or an untiring devotee, could dig deep into the mystical and poetic heart of Karol and, sifting the many little-known writings from before his pontificate, discover the Carmelite bent that saturated so many of his thoughts and prayers. It was from profound root of his spiritual life that he held so fervently that our own human communions are meant to be lifted up to reflect, and participate in, the very Triune Communion of God Himself. Michael Waldstein, in his introduction to John Paul's Theology of the Body, discovers this red thread woven through much of his works from the 1940s all the way through his pontificate, and to make the connection between this mystical experience of divine communion and Holy Communion would take little effort.[7] Or, if

---

[6] Cfr. Evert, *John Paul the Great: His Five Loves*, 139-140.

[7] Cfr. John Paul II, *Man and Woman He Created Them: A Theology of the Body*, trans. by Michael Waldstein (Boston, MA: Pauline Books & Media, 2006). See Michael Waldstein, "Introduction," 24-25: "A triangle of theses ... runs like a deeply embedded watermark through the works of Wojtyła/John Paul II, from his doctoral dissertation, *Faith according to St.*

you were looking for an even more intimate glimpse of this truth within Karol's heart, you could look back to before his ordination, when only a few years after his first attempts at poetry in the quarry outside of Krakow, now during his hidden years in the seminary, he pseudonymously published *Shores of Silence*:

God has come as far as that,

stopped but a step from nothingness,

so near our eyes.

It seemed to simple hearts,

to open hearts it seemed

that He was lost amidst the ears of corn.

And when the starved disciples husked the grains of wheat,

He waded deeper into the field.

Learn from me, my dear ones, how to hide,

for where I am hidden I abide.

John of the Cross (1948), to his last encyclical, *Ecclesia de Eucharistia* (2003). The first point on this triangle is a general account of love as a gift of self. From this point, one line extends horizontally to the thesis that the gift of self is present with particular completeness in the spousal love between man and woman. Another line extends upward diagonally, to the analogous application of the same account of love to the Trinity. Love and Gift take place in complete fullness in the begetting of the Son and the procession of the Spirit (see *Dominum et Vivificantem*, 10, just quoted above). The descending line from point three to point two represents the thesis that communion between created persons, particularly the communion of spousal love between man and woman, flows as an image from God's own trinitarian communion."

Ears of corn, lofty in your sway,

tell, do you know his hiding place?

Where should we look, tell the way

to find Him in these fertile fields.

God and the universe dwelt at the heart,

but the universe was losing light,

slowly becoming the song of His Reason,

the lowest planet.

I bring you good news of great wonder, Hellenic masters:

it is pointless to watch over existence

which slips out of our hands,

for there is a Beauty more real

concealed in the living blood.

A morsel of bread is more real

than the universe,

more full of existence, more full of the Word—

a song overflowing, the sea,

a mist confusing the sundial—

God in exile.[8]

All of these approaches would be valid and valuable ways to approach John Paul's understanding of, openness to, and relationship with the Holy Eucharist. Each of them could offer us a deepened theological and ontological understanding of the Blessed Sacrament as well as a deepened moral and personal encounter with Christ's

---

[8] Karol Wojtyła, "Shores of Silence," *Wybrzeza Pelne Ciszy*, trans. by Jerzy Peterkiewicz (Liberia Editrice Vaticana, 1944), 12-13.

sacramental Presence. However, as much as I would like to take St. Therèsè's enthusiastic "I choose all" as my motto for this essay and dive headlong into the depths that John Paul offers to us through all these different works, I would like to propose for us a different course: to consciously attempt less of a synthesis and more of a search; less an attempt to grapple and grasp the Mystery and more a choice to let ourselves be held by It. To use an image familiar to Wujek and his *Środowisko*, I think we will find it more possible, and profound, to attempt not so much a survey operation of Wojtyła, but a hiking expedition with him. It is true, if we take this path, we will not evaluate every crevice and peak, every rock and flower, of his theology, but I think that if we take this page from Karol's own playbook, we will discover that walking one particular trail with him will actually be more beautiful, rich, and transformative. Can the young Fr. Wojtyła beckon us also beyond the classroom and communists and chaos of the city, and out into creation, to have a conversation about Jesus and love, and then join him for Holy Mass on an upturned canoe?

My proposal specifically is to join, as best we can, Fr. Karol Wojtyła and his doctoral students from the Catholic University of Lublin, for their 1957 hiking trip to the Mazurian Lakes. They carried all the usual hiking gear, but also a draft of a book that their professor was working on regarding sexual and moral ethics, titled, as his doctoral lectures for the next two years would soon be called, "Love and Responsibility."[9] Herein, I propose to join with Prof.

---

[9] Cfr. George Weigel, *Witness to Hope: The Biography of Pope John Paul II*, 139. "Wojtyła's more advanced students, like Środowisko, were also a kind of laboratory for his own developing ideas. In 1957, the

Wojtyła and his students for a few days of their expedition, conversing with them about some of the chapters of his book, in particular with a glance forward towards the Mass soon to be celebrated in camp.

PART I

DO YOU HAVE A *PERSONAL* RELATIONSHIP WITH JESUS?

Chapter 1 of *Love and Responsibility* does not wait to delve into the major theme of the book:

> Man is objectively a "somebody"—and this distinguishes him from the rest of the beings of the visible world, the beings that objectively are always merely 'something.' This simple, elementary distinction conceals a deep abyss that divides the world of persons from the world of things. The

---

professor went on vacation with philosophy, psychology, and medical students in the Mazurian Lakes country of northeastern Poland. There he discussed with them the draft of a book he was writing on sexual and marital ethics, which, like his monographic lectures for the next two years, would be called Love and Responsibility. The draft text was circulated before the group left for the lake country. Each day a different student prepared a presentation on a given chapter, which the entire group then discussed and debated. According to Wojtyła's student and friend Jerzy Gałkowski, Wojtyła was not only interested in his students' judgment on the book's theoretical soundness, but also wanted to know if what he had written made sense to them practically and humanly."

objective world, to which we belong, consists of persons and things.[10]

Fr. Karol must have delved deeply into the question of what constitutes a person with his students, as he will going forward in *Love and Responsibility*, but a summary will suffice for now:

> The point in this case is not to emphasize that the person is always some unique and unrepeatable being, as this can also be stated about any other being: about an animal, a plant, or a stone. This nontransferability or incommunicability of the person is most closely linked with his interiority, with self-determination, with free will. No one else can will in my stead.[11]

In this way, Wojtyła fundamentally distinguishes persons from every other kind of thing. All of us persons are not just objects of creation; we are also *subjects*, with our own inner life and autonomy. However, persons *are also* objects in the world—they can move and change, and be moved and be changed—and some people are more vulnerable to being manipulated, *used* as Wojtyła defines this objectification, than others. "When someone else treats a person exclusively as a means to an end, then the person is violated in what belongs to his very essence and at the same time constitutes his natural

---

[10] Karol Wojtyła, *Love and Responsibility*, trans. by Grzegorz Ignatik (Boston, MA: Pauline Books & Media, 2013), 4.

[11] Ibid., 6.

right."[12] What then, is the proper disposition towards another person? Wojtyła argues that we are not only held to Kant's moral imperative of never treating another person as a means to another person's ends,[13] but also to the positive law of the Gospel, of love, "the person is a kind of good to which only love constitutes the proper and fully-mature relation."[14]

Part two of this first chapter further engages this question of how to maintain a posture of love, never use, towards another person, specifically in the male-female relationship of marriage, where only true love can uphold and safeguard each spouse's dignity and individuality against the temptation to use each other to gain pleasure or avoid pain. One particular way that the two spouses must defend their love is to choose together a common good, a common end, that extends beyond their own personal good: "this end is procreation, progeny, the family, and at the same time the whole constantly growing maturity of the relationship between both persons in all the spheres brought by the spousal relationship itself."[15] Though more will be needed than simply this recognition, such a project—an exterior good, to which you are committed with another person, which you cannot complete on your own—does lead one down the path of love. One person recognizes their need for the other, their dependence upon the other for their own completeness, and wrapped within this recognition of insufficiency and contingency is a

---

[12] Ibid., 10.
[13] Ibid., 11.
[14] Ibid., 25.
[15] Ibid., 14

simultaneous recognition of the goodness, integrity, depth, and value of the other person.[16] Love thus rises from my own interior experience of neediness, and the realization that another person can begin to fill this need, but that this other also has their own inner life and freedom and insufficiency, which I must not disregard. And thus, we find marvelously, that it is in the collision between what I might succinctly term *hungry subjects*, that love is born, and not just love, but marital love, destined for communion and covenant.

As our first afternoon's conversation thus winds down, it would naturally come to mind as we prepare for Mass that here we have all the *objects* for that sacrament—hosts, wine, water—and yet, our faith tells us that at the moment of consecration we no longer will have objects before us, but a *subject*, a person, Christ. Just like in our interactions with any person, we must never treat the Eucharist as a means to any end. Yes, we can describe the Blessed Sacrament as medicine and food, and so it is, but it is *also* a person, an encounter with another subject. Yes, Jesus does entrust Himself to us, but we must never denigrate Him to our own uses or desires. The relationship is not dissimilar from the husband who gives himself to his wife. He places his body, his heart, his future into her power, but that must not lead to her abusing their relationship, using him for the benefits or pleasures he can give to her. Vice versa, the wife allows her husband to hold her, to move her, to lead her, yet for their relationship to not devolve into one person objectifying the other, they must both hold to a loving respect of the freedom of the other, treasuring the full beauty of their personhood. Furthermore, the discovery of the

---

[16] Ibid., 32.

other's personhood is not merely a moral demand upon me, but it is at the intersection of my own autonomy, and my innate insufficiency, with another subject that my own nature is drawn into ever fuller love. Such is the case when I approach Holy Communion: my hunger draws me towards Him, but any disordered desire to take and grasp and *use* the Blessed Sacrament can be purified by the simple recognition that there I encounter there a person, not a thing. Do I approach Him just wanting some*thing* for myself, just seeking a spiritual boost, an ecstatic thrill… or do I recognize there a person to love, a relationship that itself is the end which I seek? When I receive Him, am I seeking just food for the journey, or choosing to risk my own freedom alongside of His?

<u>PART II</u>

DOES JESUS HAVE A *PERSONAL* RELATIONSHIP WITH YOU?

The second chapter of *Love and Responsibility* begins a deeper discussion of the ways and sources from which love springs up in the human heart. Wojtyła outlines three angles from which to analyze love—the metaphysical, the psychological, and the ethical—and outlines within each of these arenas various interrelated elements of love. Within the metaphysical, he examines the first foundations for human love, the interior terrain upon which love grows, and a number of paths by which from them love is gradually born, elevated, and purified for another person. He begins from simply an experience of fondness for the other, and this is already in itself a first transformation of what could simply remain a selfish urge for something desirable in the other. "Fondness, upon which this love is based, cannot be born merely from visible and sensual beauty, but should completely and thoroughly take into account the beauty of the person."[17] By cognitively, even if subconsciously, recognizing the other's personhood and choosing and willing to see them as the particular kind of good that is a *person*, not only is my affection and attraction for them protected from the unpredictability of my emotions, but this choice elevates that reaction from slipping back into a mere desire for some mere aspect of who they are.[18] In many specific ways, this repeated process of cognitively recognizing the personhood of the other and volitionally choosing to act towards them as a person, is what continues to grow love out of fondness, past a love of desire (that loves them for my own good),[19] through a benevolent love (that also desires their good),[20] to the level where sympathy evokes a subjective love for their other, and friendship commits to an objective love for the other,[21] and from here can grow to even

---

[17] Ibid., 63.

[18] Ibid., 59.

[19] Ibid., 65. "This love is manifested only as *longing for the good for oneself*: 'I want you, because you are a good for me.'"

[20] Ibid., 66. "It is not enough only to desire the person as a good for oneself, but in addition—and above all—it is also necessary to desire his good. This utterly altruistic turning of the will and affections is called in the language of St. Thomas *amor benevolentiae*, or *benevolentia*."

[21] Ibid., 74. "In friendship, however, the will commits itself. And therefore friendship really takes possession of the whole man, it is his work, it contains in itself a clear choice of the person, of the second 'I' to which it turns, while all this has not yet taken place within the limits of sympathy. The objective force of friendship consists precisely in that. Friendship,

the deepest spousal love where you give your own full person to another person with the confidence that all of each of you has been dedicated to the other's good, and finds your own good in that mutual love.[22]

All of this merely summarizes Wojtyła's metaphysical analysis of love, yet the psychological and ethical analyses can be even more succinctly considered because, as perhaps you have already noticed, a conversation with Karol Wojtyła tends to circle around a central concern, building on previous work as you gradually gain a fuller view of the topic at hand. Psychologically then, we return to the

---

however, needs to be manifested in the subject; it needs a subjective accent, as it were. And sympathy provides this. In itself sympathy is not yet friendship, although it creates conditions so that friendship between two persons can come into existence, and, once existing, can possess its subjective vividness, its climate, and its affective warmth. For the very two-sided and reciprocal 'I want the good for you,' even though it constitutes the core of friendship, remains nonetheless, so to speak, suspended in a vacuum once it is deprived of the affective warmth that sympathy provides. By no means can affection alone replace this 'I want the good for you,' which nevertheless seems cold and incommunicative when isolated from affection. From the point of view of education of love a clear postulate emerges here: sympathy must be *transformed* into friendship, and friendship *complemented* with sympathy."

[22] Ibid., 78. "Spousal love (*miłość oblubieńcza*) is something else than all the aspects or forms of love analyzed up to this point. It consists in giving one's own person. The essence of spousal love is giving oneself, giving one's 'I.' It constitutes at once something other and something more than fondness, than desire, and even than benevolence. All these forms of going out toward the other person with regard to the good do not reach as far as spousal love. 'To give oneself' means more than merely 'to want the good,' even if by that the other 'I' became as if my own, as happens in friendship."

emotional sparks from which love is kindled, and our beloved professor distinguishes the sensory impressions that first strike us of another person, and the emotional reactions that can stem from that sensory content, but which push past it into the realm of *value*. The sensory impact of an experience of another person need not dictate the emotional depth that they affect me, nor should that emotional reaction dictate the value I contemplate (and choose to uphold) in the other. A limited glimpse of my beloved from afar should not produce only a diminished delight, but also a surge of sensual attraction for someone should not commandeer my will and sweep me into a sexual liaison with them when I do not even know their name.[23] In both cases, it is my recognition that "there is another 'I,' another person" that gives direction to what could otherwise be a disordered sensual or emotional response. This is precisely the task of the ethical approach to love, which seeks not to shackle love, but to protect the heights to which love is called; not to diminish freedom, but to protect within man the fuller freedom than that found in being enslaved to his baser instincts.[24] Love is never just an experience, it is always a choice; and thus it only finds its fullness in adequately respecting the personhood of the other. Love, without taking on this

---

[23] Ibid., 84-100.

[24] Ibid., 102. "Situationism and existentialism, which supposedly in the name of freedom reject duty objectively substantiated, precisely by this very fact sever themselves from the really understood freedom of the will, or in any case from what most fully manifests this freedom. For freedom of the human will is manifested most fully in morality through duty. And duty always arises when the will encounters some norm. Hence, one cannot seek the full integration of human love in the area of psychology alone, but must look for it in ethics."

responsibility for the good of the other person, is not love at all.[25] "There exists responsibility in love—responsibility for the person, the one who is drawn into the closest community of being and acting, who in a way is made one's possession by taking advantage of his self-giving."[26]

Our first conversation emphasized the need to recognize and protect the interior life, the autonomy, the personhood of the other (and thus the person of Christ in the Eucharist). This second discussion has asked us to treasure and direct our own interior life as well: all the movements, emotions, choices, and actions that take place within me. It is by directing our hearts in accord with the personal value of the other, *and myself*, that we discover love, deepen it, and our relationship can correspond with what true love calls out of us. Once again, the Sacrament of Love need not be left out of this discussion. We begin by making a commitment to the personhood of

---

[25] Ibid., 112-113. "Responsibility for love is reduced, as is evident, to responsibility for the person, proceeding from it and also returning to it. Therefore, this responsibility is enormous. However, its magnitude can be understood only by the one who has a thorough sense of the value of the person. The one who possesses only the capacity to react to sexual values connected with the person and inhering in him, without, however, seeing the very value of the person, will continue to confuse love with erotics and will complicate his own life as well as that of others, thus ruining for himself and for them the proper sense of love and its essential 'flavor.' For this 'flavor' of love is bound with the sense of responsibility for the person. After all, this sense implies concern for the true good of the person—the quintessence of all altruism and at the same time an infallible sign of some expansion of one's 'I,' of one's existence, with this 'other I' and with this other existence, which is for me as close as my own."

[26] Ibid., 112.

Jesus, to *not* turning the Most Holy Sacrament into a means or object, and now, holding that truth high, we gently enter our own hearts. There, I suspect, all of us will find certain things that seem to clash with the truth of His personhood, and ours. Perhaps we find a raging sea of emotions—fears, uncertainties, insufficiencies… joys, attractions, desires… other interests, distractions, or relationships— that do not calm in His Presence? Maybe the limited sensory experience we have before the Sacred Host does not elucidate the joy or desire that we would like? Or do we find within ourselves frustration or anger at the Church's teachings on being properly disposed to receive Jesus, or frustration or anger at ourselves for not being who we want to be when we encounter Him, or frustration or anger at Jesus for not being Who we thought He was, or giving what we thought He would give? All of these are valid, real, true parts of our heart, and it is by the simple, continued, practice of recognizing His Person, that all of these marvelously become the substrate, the sparks, the sources that can grow into deeper and truer love for Jesus! Fears, surrendered to another person, are turned into trust and intimacy. Distractions, communicated, become conversations. Sensation, personalized, we now see as limited, but lovely, glimpses of our beloved, as if through a latticework.[27] Even anger, offered to the other while respecting their person, can be the foundation for understanding, reconciliation, and freedom.

---

[27] Song of Songs 2:9. "My beloved is like a gazelle or a young stag. Behold, there he stands behind our wall, gazing through the windows, looking through the lattice."

PART III

DOES GOD HOLD YOUR HEART? DO YOU HOLD HIS?

Chapter Three of *Love and Responsibility* has the self-acknowledged provocative title, "The Person and Chastity," beginning with a section on the "Rehabilitation of Chastity"[28] Wojtyła's concern is not just to make an apology for chastity—one of the many Christian virtues that have been neglected, and rejected—but to continue his defense of true love, and of the young people he loved so much who were setting out into the rigors of human life today. He knew their hearts would be buffeted by the attacks upon love so rampant around them.[29] "[W]e must consider very seriously," he lovingly explains, "the possibility of a *disintegration* of love. This refers to a lived-experience or even a number of amorous lived-experiences that find their source and basis in the senses and affections, while

---

[28] Karol Wojtyła, *Love and Responsibility*, trans. by Grzegorz Ignatik (Boston, MA: Pauline Books & Media, 2013), 125.

[29] George Weigel, *Witness to Hope*, 140-141. "Life under communism posed its own challenges to sexual morality and marital chastity. As payback for its 1956 concessions to the Church, the Gomułka regime instituted a permissive abortion law, a direct assault on classic Catholic morality. Youngsters on state-sponsored summer outings were encouraged to experiment with sex as another means to pry them away from the Church. The communist campaign against traditional family life had its own secondary effects on sexual morality, for the linkage the Church taught between marital love and procreation was broken if men and women came to think of children as problems to be solved rather than as gifts to be cherished. Communist materialism also contributed to a cultural climate in which sexuality became morally devalued."

themselves being still personally immature."[30] Chastity, he explains, is the virtue that parses the experiences of their heart and holds onto that which is in accord with true love, with the value of the other person, and their own value.[31] Our flesh is fallen, so the emotional and experiential content of our hearts is not an infallible guide towards love! We need something from beyond just ourselves, a virtue, a voice, a conscience, a person Who helps us on the path towards true love.

This chapter, and the following one, "Chapter IV: Justice with Respect to the Creator,"[32] explain the ways that God steps into this need, and how *He* provides the guideposts for seeking, and finding, true love. The first, one that we often find rather uncomfortable, is the experience of shame. Shame, Wojtyła earnestly explained to his students, is an interior signal, an elemental conscience, that flares up when a relationship has fallen from proper regard for the person. If we have fallen into objectifying another, or when we find ourselves objectified by them,[33] shame shakes our heart. When love displaces any kind of use in the arena of persons, shame subsides. He emphasizes that proper love does not mean that we will never feel the cold grip of shame, nor that we will never find ourselves sensually shook towards denigrating another to merely their value on one plane— affective, sexual, physical, financial, etc. —but that in both of those cases, above the shame or sensuality, our choice will continue to be one of love for them and desire for their good. Notice that what we

---

[30] Wojtyła, *Love and Responsibility*, 127.

[31] Ibid., 128-129.

[32] Ibid., 193-249.

[33] Ibid., 158-165.

have here, which fits with our deepest desire, is a consistent, practice, full love, and this is what we call the virtue of chastity. This virtue—the capacity and practice of living by the personalistic norm—beyond any practical preparations or colloquial wisdom, is the virtue that a man and woman need to have achieved before undertaking marriage.[34] They do not need *perfect* love, but they do need authentically *personal* love. Their readiness is not found in some unreachable, impeccable wholehearted gift of self; in fact, as we saw, sometimes *hole*-hearted self-gift (including the struggles and insufficiencies) is precisely what is called for. Above all, chastity means that their love must not be *half*-hearted: giving, or receiving, only some part of themselves.

A final clarification is important before we close this conversation: this interior voice that calls us to a full love of persons is not just our own intuition, nor even the deepest, truest, tendencies written on our hearts making themselves heard, it is, in fact, a word from our Creator.

> Thanks to his rationality man comprehends that he possesses himself (*sui iuris*), and at the same time that he as a creature is a possession of the Creator, and experiences (*przeżywać*) the Creator's right of ownership with respect to

---

[34] Ibid., 199. "A man and a woman whose love has not thoroughly matured, has not crystallized as a fully-mature union of persons, should not marry, for they are not prepared for the life test of marriage. In any case, the point is not for their love to be already definitively mature at the moment of contracting marriage, but to be mature for further maturation within marriage and through marriage."

himself…. For the fact of intercourse makes a person (X) become in a certain way a possession of another person (Y), and this at the same time occurs in the opposite direction: Y is a possession of X. Thus, if a need exists to justify this fact of the reciprocal relation of Y-X and X-Y, then at the same time an objective need exists to justify it with respect to the Creator…. Here we find ourselves at the threshold of understanding the "sacramentality" of marriage. According to the teaching of the Church, it is a sacrament from the beginning, i.e., from the moment of creation"[35]

Our heart's yearning back to the beginning, to relationships that uphold the full personhood of the other, is in fact a call by God, for He has designed such relationships, from the beginning, to be icons of His own love in the world. This call asks not only that we respect another human person, and have the interior capacity to entrust our own personhood to them, but also that we adequately respect the Person of God in this same way. We must uphold love in our actions—as God would have us—and abide in His love by responding to His self-gift by a corresponding self-entrustment back to Him.[36]

---

[35] Ibid., 206-207.

[36] Ibid., 232. "The more fully man knows the love of God toward himself, the more fully he also comprehends the rights that God has with regard to his person and his love. So, he sees how far-reaching human obligations are in relation to God and tries to realize them. True religion (*religijność*) consists in justice thus understood with respect to God—according to St. Thomas the virtue of religion constitutes *pars potentialis iustitiae*." Also, page 233: "Evidently, justice with respect to the Creator on

It is upon this final point that we find ourselves taking this whole conversation covering chastity and shame, and vocation and divine-reflection, back to the Holy Eucharist. Our first discovery in our walk with Karol Wojtyła was our need for a profound, *personal*, respect for Jesus' presence in that sacrament. Next we found that it was precisely in recognizing and protecting the presence of His Person in the sacrament of His body and blood that our own hearts were opened, our depths as human persons were healed, and our own misdirected love was oriented and integrated. Now, in the face of the pressures of the world that attack and denigrate true love, we find in the Eucharist the fullest manifestation of the eternal love by which God always holds us, and in which we must choose constantly to be renewed. Here, after our search, we can finally approach the Altar properly, able to receive Christ as food. If we had begun our journey simply snagging the Eucharist as a spiritual meal would have been to forget His Person, but now, holding His personal presence as fuller and closer than even our own, and healed by His Love, we can come to receive all that He is, because we are capable, and called, to give Him all that we are.

CONCLUSION

That very day two of them were going to a village named Emmaus, about seven miles from Jerusalem, and they were talking with each other about all these things that had

---

the part of man comprises two elements: the preservation of the order of nature and the manifestation of the value of the person."

happened. While they were talking and discussing together, Jesus himself drew near and went with them. But their eyes were kept from recognizing him. And he said to them, "What is this conversation that you are holding with each other as you walk?" And they stood still, looking sad. Then one of them, named Cleopas, answered him, "Are you the only visitor to Jerusalem who does not know the things that have happened there in these days?" And he said to them, "What things?" And they said to him, "Concerning Jesus of Nazareth, a man who was a prophet mighty in deed and word before God and all the people, and how our chief priests and rulers delivered him up to be condemned to death, and crucified him. But we had hoped that he was the one to redeem Israel. Yes, and besides all this, it is now the third day since these things happened. Moreover, some women of our company amazed us. They were at the tomb early in the morning, and when they did not find his body, they came back saying that they had even seen a vision of angels, who said that he was alive. Some of those who were with us went to the tomb and found it just as the women had said, but him they did not see." And he said to them, "O foolish ones, and slow of heart to believe all that the prophets have spoken! Was it not necessary that the Christ should suffer these things and enter into his glory?" And beginning with Moses and all the Prophets, he interpreted to them in all the Scriptures the things concerning himself. So they drew near to the village to which they were going. He acted as if he were going farther, but they urged him strongly, saying,

"Stay with us, for it is toward evening and the day is now far spent." So he went in to stay with them. When he was at table with them, he took the bread and blessed and broke it and gave it to them. And their eyes were opened, and they recognized him. And he vanished from their sight. They said to each other, "Did not our hearts burn within us while he talked to us on the road, while he opened to us the Scriptures?" And they rose that same hour and returned to Jerusalem. And they found the eleven and those who were with them gathered together, saying, "The Lord has risen indeed, and has appeared to Simon!" Then they told what had happened on the road, and how he was known to them in the breaking of the bread. [37]

I began this essay, and now conclude it, with a couple searching for the Lord. At first Our Lady and St. Joseph simply illustrated the enormity of the task confronting us in searching for the face of Christ in the Eucharist amidst the complete works of John Paul II. Still, like them, we stumbled upon a particular conversation between a teacher and students where we found He Whom we were looking for. Here, at the end of this meditation, I turn to the end of Luke's Gospel, to another couple, another conversation, another hiking trip, and their (also famous, if here unexpected) finding of Christ. At first they cannot see that Christ is in fact their companion, yet by simply opening their hearts to Him, and receiving His heart opened to them, they prepare the way for their subsequent, spectacular,

---

[37] Luke 24:13-35, ESVCE.

recognition of Him in the Breaking of the Bread. It was simply an encounter, a *personal* encounter, just the daily task to uphold the personal goodness of this unrecognized figure in front of them, that was a sufficient openness to the hidden God standing before them for them to eventually receive and recognize Him. The personal respect that the Eucharist asks of us was intact in their hearts when so much else had been lost or forgotten. Then, almost without knowing it, they unburdened all the brokenness and loss of their hearts to Him, and found not emptiness but fire within them. Finally, after this gradual ever-heightened personalization of their exchange, their eyes are opened to the Living Lord.[38] The love they always had for Jesus is crystalized and transformed; it is made a virtue, a voice, a

---

[38] A fuller exploration of John Paul's theology of the Eucharist would find immense fruit in comparing His three aspects of a responsible-relationship with Christ from *Love and Responsibility*— (1) Christ's personal presence, (2) our relationship with Him, and (3) the healing that is brought about in us thereby—with those that Prof. Feingold outlines in *The Eucharist: Mystery of Presence, Sacrifice, and Communion* (2018). To quote from his Introduction: "This book, conceived as a textbook for a course on the Eucharist, is structured around the three principal ends of the Eucharist. As the sacrament of love to the end, the Eucharist manifests three aspects of a supreme love of friendship: dwelling with the beloved, giving oneself in sacrifice for the beloved, and the most intimate gift of self to the beloved. Spousal love is built on these three aspects of complete self-giving. The Eucharist is the embodiment of Christ's spousal love for His Bride, and so it makes the Bridegroom present to dwell with His Bride with a love that is at once infinitely sacrificial and unitive. **The three principal themes of this book, therefore, are the Eucharist as the mystery of Christ's real presence, His sacrificial offering of Himself to the Father on our behalf, and His gift of Himself to us in Holy Communion....**"

presence that will never depart their hearts again. And they run back to Jerusalem shouting of the Lord's resurrection. And so could we.

> [E]very day, beginning on 2 November 1946, when I cele-
> brated my first Mass in the Crypt of Saint Leonard in Wawel
> Cathedral in Krakow, my eyes have gazed in recol-lection
> upon the host and the chalice, where time and space in some
> way "merge" and the drama of Golgotha is re-presented in a
> living way, thus revealing its mysterious "contemporaneity".
> Each day my faith has been able to recognize in the conse-
> crated bread and wine the divine Wayfarer who joined the
> two disciples on the road to Emmaus and opened their eyes
> to the light and their hearts to new hope.[39]

---

[39] John Paul II, Ecclesia de Eucharistia, n. 59.

Chapter 11

Fraternity, Service, and Love:
Pope Francis on the Centrality of the Eucharist

Dr. Joseph J. Plaud

"In the Eucharist, the one true God receives the greatest worship the world can give him, for it is Christ himself who is offered. When we receive Him in holy Communion, we renew our covenant with Him and allow Him to carry out ever more fully his work of transforming our lives."

- Pope Francis, *Gaudete et Exsultate: On the Call to Holiness in Today's World*[1]

Pope Francis proclaimed the celebration and the sacrifice of the Eucharist as "the heart of Christian initiation." The pope further elaborated that along with Baptism and Confirmation, the Eucharist "constitutes the source of the Church's life itself. From this Sacrament of Love, in fact, flows every authentic journey of faith, of communion, and of witness."[2] This journey of faith, communion, and witness Pope Francis articulates is fully in line

---

[1] 76-77.

[2] The Editors, "Pope Francis on the Eucharist," Adoremus, Online at https://adoremus.org/2014/04/pope-francis-on-the-eucharist

with the unbroken tradition celebrated during the past two mil-
lennia in which the Eucharist has formed the centerpoint of Catholic faith and liturgy. In churches large and small, from east to west,
this perfect sacrifice of Christ is memorialized daily. As St. Pope
John Paul II observed in his general audience of October 11, 2000,
the term "Eucharist" itself refers to "thanksgiving;" and in its essence
"the Son of God unites redeemed humanity to himself in a hymn of
thanksgiving and praise.... At the Last Supper, in order to institute
the Eucharist, Jesus gave thanks to his Father (cf. Matt 26:26-27 and
parallels); this is the origin of the name of this sacrament."[3]

The Eucharist and the Holy Catholic Church

Recounted in the Synoptic Gospels with some variation and referenced in a different context in the Gospel of John, the Eucharist as
liturgically practiced in the Catholic Mass derives from what it traditionally termed as the "Last Supper," an event which preceded the
crucifixion of Jesus, in which Christ instructed His apostles to do
something rather specific in His own memory—and, as it turns out,
for very important reasons. The Catholic liturgy itself exists as an
ever-present testament to following these words of Jesus. In this case
piecing together the Gospels of Matthew (26:26-28), Mark (14:22-
25), Luke (22:19-20), and the words of St. Paul in his First Letter to
the Corinthians (11:23-25), we have what Fortescue called "the

---

[3] L'Osservatore Romano, "The Holy Father's General Audience Address of October 11, 2000," Catholic Culture. Online at https://catholiccul-
ture.org/culture/library/view.cfm?recnum=3212

essential nucleus of the holy liturgy in any rite."[4] Although the Gospel of John neither details a Passover meal nor a Last Supper rite, in John 6:53-58 we do read the clear implications of what the Synoptic Gospels and Paul refer to in terms of the meaning of the Eucharist:

> So Jesus said to them, "Very truly, I tell you, unless you eat the flesh of the Son of Man and drink his blood, you have no life in you. Those who eat my flesh and drink my blood have eternal life, and I will raise them up on the last day; for my flesh is true food and my blood is true drink. Those who eat my flesh and drink my blood abide in me, and I in them. Just as the living Father sent me, and I live because of the Father, so whoever eats me will live because of me. This is the bread that came down from heaven, not like that which your ancestors ate, and they died. But the one who eats this bread will live forever.

Fast forward to the Catholic Mass that employs these Scriptural passages in its own development, and there are two major elements, typically referred to as the Liturgy of the Word and the Liturgy of the Eucharist. Spiritual nourishment at the table of the Lord begins with holy Scripture (Liturgy of the Word), followed by the Eucharistic sacrifice (Liturgy of the Eucharist). As Pope Benedict XVI summarized:

---

[4] Adrian Fortescue, *The Mass: A Study of Roman Liturgy* (New York: Longmans, Green and Co., 1914), p. 1.

From listening to the word of God, faith is born or strength-
ened (cf. Rom 10:17); in the Eucharist the Word made flesh
gives himself to us as our spiritual food. Thus, from the two
tables of the word of God and the Body of Christ, the Church
receives and gives to the faithful the bread of life…Conse-
quently it must constantly be kept in mind that the word of
God, read and proclaimed by the Church in the liturgy, leads
to the Eucharist as to its own connatural end.[5]

Therefore, in the Catholic context at least, we have a long-estab-
lished central component of the Holy Mass, the Liturgy of the Eucharist, in which the faithful partake in a ritual of thanksgiving by
receiving the literal body and blood of the Lord Jesus Christ, the
transformed bread and wine through the intercession of the Holy
Spirit, in a sacred process termed *transubstantiation.*

It is the case therefore that during the Catholic Mass the bread
becomes the Body and the wine the Blood of Christ; not as symbols,
not as a mere presence, but in essence the actual body and blood of
the Savior. It is for this reason that when the priest distributes communion to the faithful at Mass, he does not say "this is the bread,"
but "the body of Christ.[6]

---

[5] Pope Benedict XVI, "Sacramentum Caritatis" (Post-Synod Exhortation on the Eucharist as the Source and Summit of the Church's Life and
Mission). Online at https://www.vatican.va/

[6] Kjetil Kringlebotten. *Do This in Remembrance of Me: The Sacrificial
Aspect of the Eucharist in the Systematic Theology of Wolfhart Pannenberg
and Joseph Ratzinger* (Master's Thesis in Christian Studies, NLA University College, Bergen, 2012), p. 6.

Service, Sacrifice and Love: Eucharistic Essence in Practice

Pope Francis focuses precisely on the Eucharist as the fulcrum of Catholic faith because the "Eucharist is the synthesis of the entire existence of Jesus, which was a single act of love for the Father and his brothers… [it is] the sacrament of His Body and His Blood given for the salvation of the world."[7] So in the pope's theology the Eucharist is not only the entire expression of the divinity of Christ on earth, but the Holy Father goes a step further in directly linking the Eucharist to Christ's love and our salvation. In Pope Francis's theological lexicon, the Eucharist is not just "a thing," meaning the divine body and blood of Christ, but it is also a process, a transformational transitive verb in which the very nature of the Lord becomes the expression of pure love and our very salvation in communion with God. In this way Pope Francis gives us a natural and more modern version of St. Paul's preaching that equated the Eucharist not only with the literal body of Christ as offered by Jesus at the Last Supper, but also with the Church itself as the body of the risen Christ: "Now you are Christ's body, and individually parts of it" (1 Corinthians 12:27).

In Pope Francis's view, the celebration of the Eucharist becomes for Catholics not only the literal sacrifice of the Savior upon the cross in death; but in a joyous manner it is the very essence of the Church itself, in which we become as one with the body of Christ: "As a body is one though it has many parts, and all the parts of the

---

[7] Courtney Mares, "Pope Francis: The Eucharist is Jesus Alive," Catholic News Agency. Online at https://www.catholicnewsagency.com/news/41618/ pope-francis-the-eucharist-is-jesus-alive

body, though many, are one body, so also Christ. For in one Spirit we were all baptized into one body, whether Jews or Greeks, slaves or free persons, and we were all given to drink of one Spirit" (1 Corinthians 12:12-13). For Pope Francis, the celebration of the Eucharist embodies the very presence of Christ in our lives here on earth, what he has termed "Jesus alive."[8] Drawing again upon the words of St. Paul as detailed in 1 Corinthians 6:12-19, Pope Francis articulates that through the Eucharist we unite ourselves to God, we break out of our human limitations, blending divinity with humanity, and experience the reality of the living Christ today. This union with Christ is only possible in the pope's emphasis because of the Incarnation and God's infinite love through the passion and crucifixion, and Christ's triumph over death in the resurrection. We are directly bound to Jesus through the Eucharist.

The Eucharist and Transubstantiation

Pope Francis has also been a strong and direct advocate in another important domain: Eucharistic integrity in the eyes and hearts of the faithful. The troubling fact of the matter is that in the present world—including among most Catholics—there is questioning concerning the true presence of Christ in the Eucharist; a questioning of the very validity of transubstantiation itself. If unchallenged, this troubling trend has the potential to influence in a pernicious manner the very essence of the Eucharistic celebration which forms the

---

[8] Ibid.

cornerstone of not only Holy Mass, but of the sacramental Church itself.

A 2019 Pew Research Center report found that only a third of American Catholics agreed with transubstantiation, meaning that the Eucharist is the body and blood of Christ. A sizable majority of Catholics stated rather that they believed the bread and wine served symbolic purposes instead of becoming the body and blood of Christ during Holy Mass.[9] In this domain Pope Francis has been equally forceful in his message to the world on the nature of the Eucharist:

> It is the body of Jesus; it finished there! Faith: faith comes to our aid; with an act of faith, we believe that it is the body and blood of Christ.... The action of the Holy Spirit and the efficacy of Christ's own words uttered by the priest make truly present, in the form of bread and wine, His Body and His Blood, His sacrifice offered on the cross once and for all.... Jesus was very clear about this.[10]

In 1 Corinthians 10:1-22, St. Paul instructs us that the one bread makes us into one body. It is the very life of the Church that is the embodiment of this unity created by Communion, the unity of all

---

[9] Gregory A. Smith, "The Pew Research Center: Just One-Third of U.S. Catholics Agree with Their Church that Eucharist is Body, Blood of Christ," Pew Research. Online at https://www.pewresearch.org/fact-tank/2019/08/ 05/transubstantiation-eucharist-u-s-catholics/.

[10] Kathleen N. Hattrup, "The Eucharist IS Jesus, Just Have Faith: Pope Francis," Aleteia. Online at https://aleteia.org/2018/03/07/the-eucharist-is-jesus-just-have-faith-pope-francis/.

members of the Body of Christ (the Church) through the one Christ. Also, as we read in 1 Corinthians 11:17-33, it is the Eucharist that gathers the Church together as one body, one spirit in Christ—how more central to the life of the Church can anything else be? Pope Francis enlarges on the centrality of this theme when he notes that the celebration of the Eucharist both fosters fraternity and is the conduit to our very holiness and service to others as a missionary community.

The pope also explains that the Eucharist is what "gives rise to authentic and shared mystical experiences."[11] The Eucharist creates for the Church in its people a blood relationship, a sharing of blood with Christ and with each other as Catholics. In Pope Francis's Eucharistic focus, Christ, though broken and vulnerable in his Passion, out of fragility emerges ultimate love, ultimate sharing, and the giving of oneself to others.[12] This overarching theme of the Eucharist as "a dynamism of sacrificial love," which allows us to "become persons of peace, forgiveness, reconciliation and sharing in solidarity," is the consistent and central theme promulgated by Pope Francis throughout his Pontificate.[13]

---

[11] Pope Francis, (2018, March 19). *Gaudete et Exsultate: On the Call to Holiness in Today's World*, §142. Online at https://www.vatican.va/

[12] Linda Bordoni. "Pope at Angelus: The Eucharist is the Bread of Sinners Not a Reward of Saints," Vatican News. Online at https://www.vaticannews.va/en/pope/news/2021-06/pope-angelus-corpus-christi-catechesis-eucharist.html

[13] Elise Harris, "Pope Francis: Let Yourself Be Transformed by the Eucharist," Catholic News Agency. Online at https://www.catholicnewsagency.com/news/32481/pope-francis-let-yourself-be-transformed-by-the-eucharist.

Pope Francis and Current Issues Concerning Eucharistic Practices within the Church

The ability of individual Catholics to participate actively in the Eucharistic celebration and receive Communion has been challenged in some cases by local Church authorities. Further, Catholics who divorce and remarry without first obtaining an annulment prior to subsequent marriage are also forbidden by Canon Law to receive the Eucharist, as the Church basically considers this to be an adulterous situation in which the civilly remarried Catholic is not currently in a state of grace. Presuming as we do here that where the Eucharist is celebrated there lies the Church, both in respect to the individual churches celebrating the Sacrament and the worldwide Church as a whole, it is no wonder that differences have emerged in thought and opinion concerning the circumstances Catholics may be forbidden or otherwise questioned concerning reception of Communion. As the *Catechism of the Catholic Church* reminds us in §1436,

> daily conversion and penance find their source and nourishment in the Eucharist, for in it is made present the sacrifice of Christ which has reconciled us with God. Through the Eucharist those who live from the life of Christ are fed and strengthened. "It is a remedy to free us from our daily faults and to preserve us from mortal sins."[14]

---

[14] Catholic Church, *Catechism of the Catholic Church*, 2nd ed. (Our Sunday Visitor, 2000).

Let us take a bit of a detour here to explore some of the more technical issues involving the nature of the Eucharist that have implications regarding the current controversies concerning participation in the Eucharistic celebration at Holy Mass by individual Catholics. St. Thomas Aquinas makes several critical distinctions concerning three elements or features notable in the sacraments: (1) the *sacramentum tantum*, or the outward sign or the sacramental rite itself, which is not itself caused but brings about other things; (2) the *res tantum*, which is the sacramental grace that is imparted through the sacramentum tantum; and (3) the *res et sacramentum*, the symbolic reality element itself caused by the sacramentum tantum, which itself also marks and causes the *res tantum* along with the *sacramentum tantum*. St. Thomas himself illustrates the significance of all three elements in the sacrament of the Holy Eucharist:

> The effect of this Sacrament is twofold: first, in the very consecration of the Sacrament, since in virtue of the above words bread is changed into the Body of Christ, and wine into His Blood; so that Christ is entirely contained under the appearances of bread which remain without a subject; and Christ is entirely contained under the appearances of wine. And, moreover, under each part of the consecrated Host and of the consecrated wine, Christ is totally present even after the separation is made. The second effect of this Sacrament brought about in the soul of one who worthily receives is the union of man with Christ, as He himself says: "He who eats My Flesh, and drinks My Blood, abides in Me, and I in him." And since man is incorporated with Christ and united to His

members through grace, it follows that through this Sacrament grace is increased in those who receive it worthily. Thus, therefore, in this Sacrament there is that which is the Sacrament alone ("sacramentum tantum"), that is, the species of bread and wine; and that which is known as the "res et sacramentum," that is, the true Body of Christ; and that which is the "res tantum," that is the unity of the Mystical Body, that is, the Church which this Sacrament both signifies and causes.[15]

The significance of this understanding of the Eucharist is explicated nicely in the *Catechism of the Catholic Church* in §1128:

This is the meaning of the Church's affirmation that the sacraments act ex opere operato (literally: "by the very fact of the action's being performed"), i.e., by virtue of the saving work of Christ, accomplished once for all. It follows that "the sacrament is not wrought by the righteousness of either the celebrant or the recipient, but by the power of God." From the moment that a sacrament is celebrated in accordance with the intention of the Church, the power of Christ and his Spirit acts in and through it, independently of the personal holiness of the minister. *Nevertheless, the fruits of the sacra-*

---

[15] St. Thomas Aquinas, *The Catechetical Instructions of St. Thomas.* EWTN. Online at https://www.ewtn.com/catholicism/library/catechetical-instructions-of-st-thomas-12545

ments also depend on the disposition of the one who receives them [emphasis added].[16]

Ex opere operato, derived from Latin meaning "by the work worked," essentially means that through the working of the Holy Spirit, the sacraments confer grace upon those receiving them through God, *when the sign is validly affected.* In no way is the imparting of grace the result of the person receiving grace, it is imparted wholly by the power and love of God: *ex opere operantis.* This term, derived from Latin meaning "from the work of the one working," *refers to the good dispositions or the merits of the person performing them.* This is to be distinguished from the *ex opere operato* as defined above, which concerns the conferring of grace upon those receiving the sacraments through the power and love of God. *Ex opere operantis* also can refer to any number of factors or situations that can determine *how much of God's grace is received by a person who approaches the sacraments with personal piety, the faith of the person, or the performance of good works.*

Why does all this matter to the current debates and controversies surrounding who should and who should not receive Communion? Put directly, the magisterium of the Catholic Church expresses through its teaching authority that any Catholic wishing to participate in the celebration of the Eucharist and therefore receive Communion at Holy Mass should not be conscious of any grave sin and that person should have fasted for one hour prior to its reception.

---

[16] Catholic Church, *Catechism of the Catholic Church,* 2nd ed. (Our Sunday Visitor, 2000).

As the early Christian philosopher and writer St. Justin Martyr noted in the mid-second century A.D. in his *First Apology*:

> And this food is called among us Εὐχαριστα [the Eucharist], of which no one is allowed to partake but the man who believes that the things which we teach are true, and who has been washed with the washing that is for the remission of sins, and unto regeneration, and who is so living as Christ has enjoined.[17]

Beyond individual Catholics who personally find themselves in a state of grave sin, certain public figures—especially those who serve in government—have also encountered Eucharistic prohibition by Church authorities on local levels. Controversies in this latter domain have only been accelerating as of late. The teaching authority of the Church should not be diminished in any capacity, and such authority ultimately resides with the local bishop. The focus of the present chapter centers instead on the approach of Pope Francis to issues involving reception of Communion. The Holy Father has been very direct in his pastoral approach in addressing the significant issue of which Catholic should or should not be allowed to participate in the Eucharistic celebration.

---

[17] Justin Martyr, *The First Apology*, Bible Hub. Online at https://biblehub.com/library/richardson/early_christian_fathers/the_first_apology_of_justin.htm.

The Pastoral Approach to the Eucharist Exemplified by Pope Francis

Insight into Pope Francis's pastoral approach to participating in the sacraments of the Church, principally in the Eucharistic celebration, was seen in his Apostolic Exhortation *Amoris Laetitia* (The Joy of Love). The eighth chapter of the exhortation, entitled "Accompanying, Discerning and Integrating Weakness," delves into the issue of Communion for divorced and remarried Catholics. In a footnote in this chapter Pope Francis notes, "I would also point out that the Eucharist 'is not a prize for the perfect, but a powerful medicine and nourishment for the weak.'"[18] A key to understanding the approach taken by Pope Francis in this chapter, and most notably in the above-quoted footnote, is that it does not represent a blanket approval extended to those who are civilly remarried to obtain Communion. The focus here is rather on a process of discernment. As Ryan notes,

> Clearly, the Pope is not giving a blanket permission for those divorced and remarried extra-ecclesia to receive Holy Communion. Such a step can only be the result of a personal discernment before God, made within the internal forum, within an ecclesial setting (with one's pastor or spiritual guide) and put into practice with humility and discretion."[19]

---

[18] Pope Francis, *Amoris Laetitia*. Online at https://www.vatican.va/

[19] Thomas Ryan, "'Weakness, and Wounded and Troubled Love' in *Amoris Laetitia*: Pope Francis as Pastor," *Australasian Catholic Record*, 94 (2), 131-147, 2017.

In this approach we see Pope Francis not foreclosing the possibility for those out of step with Church teachings, in this case divorce and remarriage, to receive the sacraments, most notably Communion, but it isn't an automatic permission statement; rather, it's a call to discernment. As cogently summarized by Pedro Gabriel: "The Eucharist may be given to those in irregular situations who, on account of mitigating factors diminishing subjective culpability, are not in a state of mortal sin."[20] Just as importantly, what Pope Francis is seeking to accomplish in this pastoral fashion is to provide for a means by which those in irregular circumstances as such have the time and space in the grace conferred through the sacrament to reach for the moral ideal. In a follow-up letter written to Bishop Sergio Alfredo Fenoy of San Miguel, Argentina, in September 2016, Francis wrote that pastoral charity "moves us to reach out to those who have drifted away, and once we have met them, to begin a path of welcoming, accompaniment, discernment and integration into the ecclesial community."[21]

Pope Francis has also extended this pastoral approach to the political arena in which certain Catholic politicians have been denied access to the Eucharist. In September 2022, while returning from a papal visit to central Europe Francis pointedly stated that he himself never denied the Eucharist to any person, emphasizing that the

---

[20] Pedro Gabriel, *The Orthodoxy of Amoris Laetitia* (Wipf and Stock Publishers, 2022), p. 54.

[21] Catholic News Agency, "What Pope Francis Said About Communion for the Divorced-and-Remarried." Online at https://www.catholic-newsagency.com/news/34544/what-pope-francis-said-about-communion-for-the-divorced-and-remarried

pastoral response would be in his judgment the most appropriate one: "If we look at the history of the Church, we can see that every time the bishops did not act like shepherds when dealing with a problem, they aligned themselves with political life, on political problems."[22]

Conclusion: Pope Francis Sees the Eucharist as the Glue to Universal Love and Service

During the pontificate of Pope Francis, there are numerous examples in both his writings and public speeches that the pope puts the Eucharist at the very center of the life of the Catholic Church. Although publications such as *Amoris Laetitia have caused some to question whether Pope Francis was departing in a significant manner from established Church orthodoxy, quite to the contrary, the pope's approach in this domain has been one that emphasizes the centrality of the Eucharist in daily Catholic life as the springboard to a life of Christian fellowship and love, and ultimately redemption.*

Pope Francis identifies the Eucharist as the truest and surest way in which Jesus Christ joins His own divine life to ours. To this pope, the Eucharist is not a reward of the saints; it is the bread of the sinners. The Eucharist is the binding agent between our mortal lives and the divine, the ultimate invitation for us to participate as one body of Christ in Christ. Participation in the Eucharistic feast

---

[22] Claire Giangravé, "Pope Francis Addresses the Communion Ban: 'I Have Never Denied the Eucharist to Anyone!'", Religion News Service. Online at https://religionnews.com/2021/09/15/pope-francis-addresses-the-communion-ban-i-have-never-denied-the-eucharist-to-anyone/

propels us forward in love as Christians and is the guidepost to our salvation.

To Pope Francis, joining ourselves to Christ does not come at the expense of isolating ourselves from others. Rather, it is an invitation to encounter and engage with others. The Eucharist is our heavenly food to nourish and guide us on the path to this Christian fellowship. In the final analysis, "The Church does not rest solely beneath the shadow of our steeple; rather, she embraces a vast number of peoples and nations who profess the same faith, are nourished by the same Eucharist, and are served by the same pastors. To feel that we are in communion with the whole Church, with all of the Catholic communities of the world great and small! This is beautiful!"[23]

---

[23] Pope Francis. (2013, October 9). General Audience. *The Church of Mercy.* Online at https://www.vatican.va/

www.ingramcontent.com/pod-product-compliance
Lightning Source LLC
Chambersburg PA
CBHW070028100426
42740CB00013B/2630